Beloved Warrior
Love is the Weapon

Gail Dixon

Copyright © 2019 Gail Dixon

All rights reserved.

ISBN : 978-1-0912448-4-9

Unless otherwise indicated, all Scripture quotations are from The ESV® Bible (The Holy Bible, English Standard Version®), copyright © 2001 by Crossway, a publishing ministry of Good News Publishers. Used by permission. All rights reserved.

Scripture taken from The Message. Copyright © 1993, 1994, 1995, 1996, 2000, 2001, 2002. Used by permission of NavPress Publishing Group.

Scripture quotations marked TPT are from The Passion Translation®. Copyright © 2017, 2018 by Passion & Fire Ministries, Inc. Used by permission. All rights reserved. ThePassionTranslation.com

Scriptures taken from the Holy Bible, New International Version®, NIV®. Copyright © 1973, 1978, 1984, 2011 by Biblica, Inc.™ Used by permission of Zondervan. All rights reserved worldwide. www.zondervan.com The "NIV" and "New International Version" are trademarks registered in the United States Patent and Trademark Office by Biblica, Inc.

Scripture quotations from The Authorized (King James) Version. Rights in the Authorized Version in the United Kingdom are vested in the Crown. Reproduced by permission of the Crown's patentee, Cambridge University Press.

Copy edited and proofread by Abigail Tuddenham.
abigail.tuddenham@outlook.com

To my mother, Mavis Patricia Dixon.
My model and inspiration in love and faithfulness.

CONTENTS

	Introduction	 9
1	Drawn by the Beloved Warrior	 13
2	Resting in the Beloved Warrior	 29
3	Listening to the Beloved Warrior	 49
4	Worshipping the Beloved Warrior	 75
5	Praying in the Beloved Warrior	 101
6	Being the voice of the Beloved Warrior	 119
7	Standing in the Beloved Warrior	 145
8	Persevering in the Beloved Warrior	 169
9	Faithful in the Beloved Warrior	 189
10	Surrender to the Beloved Warrior	 211
	Epilogue	 235

Beloved Warrior
Love is the Weapon

Introduction

We live in an age of pain and promise. The pain of a suffering world that daily sees more abuse and injustice. Yet the promise that we already see in part: in the last days the Lord will pour out His Spirit on all flesh.[1]

Jesus spoke of our times and said, "And because lawlessness will be increased, the love of many will grow cold".[2]

This book is a call to stir up our love for the Lord and for each other. Jesus is the Beloved Warrior. His weapon is Himself, for He is love. The more we know Him, the more we too become beloved warriors. He trains us to fight as He fights, as lambs who, in the end, will defeat every roaring lion.

Hang my locket around your neck,
wear my ring on your finger.

---

1. Joel 2:28-29
2. Matthew 24:12

Love is invincible facing danger and death.
Passion laughs at the terrors of hell.
The fire of love stops at nothing -
it sweeps everything before it.
Flood waters can't drown love,
torrents of rain can't put it out.
Love can't be bought, love can't be sold -
it's not to be found in the marketplace.[3]

Love wins!

---

3. Song of Songs 8:6-8, The Message

Beloved warrior

Chapter 1
Drawn by the Beloved Warrior

Treasured one, what voice describes me so?
Lacking so much, so needy, this I know.
I look into Your eyes and look away,
It hurts to see Your love.

Tender, You lift my face to gaze again.
No words, but You reach deep into my pain.
A waterfall of love flows out to me
And I begin to see.

It's not my prayer, my work that You desire,
It's me! It's me you want. O Holy Fire,
Your eyes burn deep and wound me with Your love,
Sweet wounds that set me free.

You take me to Your table, there we eat.
I am enfolded. In Your love we meet.
Defences fall as I receive Your love
And sit with You, and eat.

Our Lord the passionate warrior

Jesus is in love with you! Not with a love that will burn for a time and then die, like so many relationships these days, but with the eternal flame of love that will never diminish. A love that has spoken with action. A love that has paid the price. A warrior's love.

He is the Beloved Warrior described in Exodus 15:3: *The Lord is a warrior; the Lord is his name.*[1]

In His fierce love for His oppressed people, He led them out of slavery. He parted the Red Sea with His hand outstretched over Moses' hand. Together they held the wooden staff, a type of the cross on which He would stretch out His arms for the deliverance of all mankind when the time was right.

He is still stretching out His hand today with the same passionate love, to rescue all who are oppressed by the lies of the enemy, whether they are victim or perpetrator. He completely defeated Satan and his hordes when He died on the cross. Yet much of the world still lives in bondage. He is calling His bride to rise into who she is, and become like Him, a warrior wielding the most powerful weapon of all: love.

Covenant love

He made a covenant relationship with us when we

---

1. Exodus 15:3, NIV

accepted Him as saviour. He speaks of that covenant relationship when He is preparing His disciples for His death:

"Let not your hearts be troubled. Believe in God; believe also in me. In my Father's house are many rooms. If it were not so, would I have told you that I go to prepare a place for you? And if I go and prepare a place for you, I will come again and will take you to myself, that where I am you may be also".[2]

This is the language of the bridegroom. In biblical Jewish culture, after the couple makes a covenant of betrothal together, the husband-to-be goes to prepare a place for his bride in his father's household. The couple at this stage is set apart (consecrated) for each other, but the marriage is not yet consummated. Time passes when the two are separated, but joined in their love and commitment. The bridegroom then returns with great celebration and takes his bride in a triumphal procession, along with all the gifts that people have given them, to his father's house. There is dancing, joy cries, music and song.

All of this is underlying Jesus' words. His disciples would have recognised the love language. The commitment Jesus was making to them (and now to us) was one of betrothal. He is promising a final second coming, when He will arrive in great triumph and celebration and take us, as His bride, to His Father's house. Yet He was also speaking of a very present

---

2. John 14:1-3

reality. We can know the Father, and be with Him where He is now.

> *"I am the way, and the truth, and the life. No one comes to the Father except through me. If you had known me, you would have known my Father also. From now on you do know him and have seen him."*[3]

This betrothal is not confined to time and space. There is a spiritual reality ignited in us when we enter into relationship with the One who is the Way. It is a mystery that we have eternity to explore. We enter into a knowing and a seeing of the triune God!

When Jesus uses this imagery of betrothal it is not a male/female concept. It is the Son of God attempting to help His followers to understand the greatest truth in the universe: that we are loved with an everlasting love. The Lord longs to be joined with us in a deeper way than human language could ever express, yet He wants us to understand His heart. The nearest human expression would be betrothal and marriage.

We are born again into this betrothal relationship. We thought we chose Him, but we find that He has already chosen us! Why did He choose us? The only reason He gives us is the one that He gave His people Israel. Perhaps it is the only reason that comes near to making sense of His heart... He loves us because He loves us; He is Love.

---

3. John 14:6-7

"It was not because you were more in number than any other people that the Lord set his love on you and chose you, for you were the fewest of all peoples, but it is because the Lord loves you."[4]

The betrothal

The purpose of the betrothal is a sanctification of the couple; they set themselves apart for each other. This is what the Bible means when it speaks of holiness. Jesus said, ***"And for their sake I consecrate myself, that they also may be sanctified in truth".***[5]

In the betrothal ceremony the bride price would be agreed. A cup of wine would be shared to seal the covenant that was being made. The wine represented the virgin blood that would be shed on the marriage bed as the bride and groom became one flesh.

Does all this begin to sound familiar? At the Last Supper, Jesus took the cup and made the covenant of betrothal with us. At that time, He formally agreed what the bride price would be. The wine did indeed represent blood that would be shed for the couple to become one flesh. However, this bride had already prostituted herself to other gods. So to seal the covenant, the bridegroom would shed His own lifeblood for His bride.

---

4. Deuteronomy 7:7-8

5. John 17:19

"This cup that is poured out for you is the new covenant in my blood."[6]

Our covenant is ratified under the ultimate banner of love, it is made in Jesus' own flesh.

*Therefore, brothers, since we have confidence to enter the holy places by the blood of Jesus, by the new and living way that he opened for us **through the curtain, that is, through his flesh,** and since we have a great priest over the house of God, let us draw near with a true heart in full assurance of faith, with our hearts sprinkled clean from an evil conscience and our bodies washed with pure water.*[7]

He told them, *"I go to prepare a place for you"*.[8] What preparation He made! The place He has prepared for us is in His own body. The only way we could enter into the heavenly realms and stand before our Father God is in Christ. As the rock of old was cleft for Moses that he might see the glory of God, so the Rock, Jesus, was cleft for us.

In Christ

The centurion's spear pierced into the very heart of Jesus. How do we know this?

---

6. Luke 22:20

7. Hebrews 10:19-22, emphasis added

8. John 14:2

*But one of the soldiers pierced his side with a spear, and at once there came out **blood and water.***[9]

Doctors now know that if the heart ruptures, blood leaks into a membrane that surrounds the heart called the pericardial sac. As it sits there, the blood separates from the plasma, which is clear like water. Jesus did not die as a result of the crucifixion, but because of a broken heart. It broke as He was separated from His Father for that only and awful time while He bore my sins and yours.

The place Jesus has prepared for us is not only in His body, but in His very heart. He literally opened His heart for us to come in.

He told His disciples that *"if I go and prepare a place for you, I will come again and will take you to myself"*.[10] In the wonder of the spiritual realm we discover that He is here, by the power of His Holy Spirit. We now have an amazing invitation from our warrior bridegroom. *Will you live in Me? I want us to be so close that I am willing to take you into My very heart. I want us to move as one, My heart to your heart.*

Holding hands

So, how does that work for us now? What does that mean? How can we live *in Christ*? If you are anything like me,

---

9. John 19:34, emphasis added

10. John 14:3

we slip in and out of that place of abiding. I just need to reflect back on the day to realise that some of the things I have been so concerned with may not have been so very important to Jesus.

Don't get me wrong, He is interested in every aspect of our lives. He never leaves us. He always cares for us, even when we are totally oblivious to Him. However, He is longing for a two-way relationship: *"Abide in Me, and I in you"*.[11]

If I let go of His hand, He is still holding mine, so He is with me. However, I am not in co-operation with Him. He will not drag me along behind Him like a naughty child. He wants us to walk together. He will wait for me, stay with me, but He is really longing for me to go with Him. I cannot make progress unless I walk in step with Him. The bride must leave her own family and go with the bridegroom to his. Jesus says it this way:

"If anyone would come after me, let him deny himself and take up his cross daily and follow me. For whoever would save his life (psyche) will lose it, but whoever loses his life (psyche) for my sake will save it. For what does it profit a man if he gains the whole world and loses or forfeits himself?"[12]

---

11. John 15:4

12. Luke 9:23-25

When we are with Him, we find our true selves. We find our identity and therefore begin to understand our destiny. He is the I AM. In His identity we find our little 'I am's. He has promised to take us to *Himself*, into all that He is. We came from Him. It therefore makes sense that we find our true selves again in Him. However, we have a choice. Will we lose our 'home', our *psyche*, to go with Him to His home of abundant life?

This *psyche* is what we often think of as our soul: our mind, emotions and will. It is hard to let it go, because we feel that we will lose our identity if we do so. Yet we need to trust that Jesus loves our *psyche* too. He created it. Each of us is unique, formed in His image. Although that image is marred, each one of us is still recognisable as someone precious and valuable.

However, if we try to save our *psyche* in our own strength we will lose it, because we don't really understand it. Our *psyche* was created in God's image, but we look at it through man's lens. In our earthly 'home' we judge ourselves by what others say and think, or by what we feel we should achieve or be. Our measures are bound by what we can see and understand: how much we have, how well we are educated, what we have accomplished or can accomplish.

The world has pursued knowledge; knowledge gives us the ability to live without God, or at least without reference to Him. That choice was made right from the beginning in the garden of Eden. Jesus is drawing us again to life, to the tree of life. So He says in effect:

If you want to follow me, leave this world's value system, and come and find the truth that you were created for. However, as you do this you will know a great cost. The world that you are rejecting will hate you. You will have to carry a cross daily; it is the cost of being different, the cost of loving unconditionally. It is a small part of the cross I bore. Yet if you will do this, you will really find your true self. Your true identity is worth more than the whole created world. I value each individual psyche more than everything else I ever created. I value your psyche and I died to show you the reality of my words.

Jesus' teaching about dying opens up to us the reality of true living. As we die to our old nature (trusting Jesus' word and way rather than our own) we discover a mystery in ourselves. Our life is our *psyche* and yet more than our *psyche*. We also have a spirit that bursts with life in the presence of Jesus. If we submit our life to the leading of the Holy Spirit, our own spirit can teach our soul how to view things.

Our spirit is able to respond to the Holy Spirit, rejoicing in all that is good, and sensing the ways of God. The more we 'lose' our *psyche*, the more our spirit can take the lead. Amazingly our minds, emotions and decision-making abilities all flourish when our spirit is in control. Spirit, soul and body is the biblical order of precedence. We should not simply be led by our physical needs, nor by our own thoughts and emotions, but by the Holy Spirit speaking into our spirits.

> *Now may the God of peace himself sanctify you completely, and may your whole **spirit and soul and body** be kept blameless at the coming of our Lord Jesus Christ.*[13]

Jesus knows that we cannot make good on our choice to lose our psyche without help. That is why these words of His are so very sweet: *"I will come again and will take you to myself".*[14] He comes to us again and again in the power of His Holy Spirit. He pursues us with His relentless love. As we receive the Spirit, time and time and time again, He leads us into the very heart of our saviour.

Love is patient. Love is long-suffering. He whispers to me as He gently holds my hand, *I have come, let Me take you to Myself. I am where you are, but I want you to be where I am. Let go of your own ways, and trust Me.*

Choices

The hurt in my father's eyes spoke more eloquently than all the words he had used to express how let down he

---

13. 1 Thessalonians 5:23, emphasis added

14. John 14:3

felt, how disappointed. I was his only daughter, his oldest child, graduating in a few months, the first in the family to get a degree. He'd worked hard so that I could have that opportunity to study and get on in life. He wanted me to have all the luxuries he'd had to forgo to get me through university.

We'd dreamed of a little sailboat, probably just a Mirror dinghy but something we could sail together once I had a good job and could afford half the mooring and club fees with him.

Now here I was, telling him that God had called me to North Africa!

No salary, no prospects, and it was dangerous wasn't it? A Muslim country.
And who was I going with? Just another girl my own age who was throwing her degree away too.

We weren't even being sent by a recognised group, just some upstart youth team. His blood surged, turning hurt to anger.

Who was it that was ruining his daughter's life, filling her head with lies about a God that would send her into danger? Surely, if God existed He would look after the ones who believed in Him. It should be against the law for someone to prey on young women and fill their heads with nonsense.

My heart ached. How could I explain to him what I felt? The excitement, the fear, the sense of purpose, the love? How could I show him the veiled faces and empty eyes that had seared their image in my heart and my prayer. More than that, how could I introduce my father to the One who had drawn me to His side? The One who had stolen my heart with His acceptance, His forgiveness and His unconditional love? All I knew was that I had to pursue this love that I had found. Nothing else made sense any more.

Three years later...

I watched as my father smiled at the kids who flocked around him, this tall greying foreigner. They pressed their grubby hands into his trouser legs, each vying for his attention. A town official came and chased them away. "We are very happy you sent us your daughter", I blushed as I translated for my father.

The visit was everything I could have dreamed of. My parents fell in love with the country. It seemed that everyone was on their best behaviour. They were invited for so many meals they thought they would burst. One friend said with joy, "Now we know that you are like us, you have parents too!"

Gradually my friend and I were building meaningful friendships. Sometimes it was in our weakness that most progress was made. Our friends had discovered that we cried like them, that we could argue like them, and get annoyed and impatient like them. However, they also discovered that, unlike them, we had learned how to forgive.

When we told one friend the story of the Prodigal Son, she interrupted at the critical moment when the son was returning to the father and said, "and he hit him and hit him and hit him!"

She was absolutely stunned to learn of the Father's forgiveness. Today she knows that forgiveness for herself, as do others whom we befriended.

Today my own father is in heaven, his heart wooed and melted by the same unconditional love that had won his daughter.

Chapter 2
Resting in the Beloved Warrior

When my heart's torn, I cling to You
I feel Your hands, Your side.
I find my peace within Your arms
And make Your gentle grip my joy,
I find the place to hide.

A place of rest within the Rock
Within Your opened side.
A place to learn the ways of God,
To hear Your name; Compassion, Love
And Justice glorified.

Your name now whispered, now proclaimed
I hear as You pass by,
And there my ache, my pain is met
And I take courage yet again
Within the Crucified.
In Your pierced heart I find my rest,
Your scars my healing bring,

And in Your Name my hope springs new
I love because You love, and You
Have more to gather in.

I AM, I AM, and I WILL BE
The LORD, the One who cares.
Draw near, don't doubt, simply believe.
Come now and touch My torn side
And find your wholeness there.

Now that He has drawn us to Himself, now that we've caught a glimpse of His beauty, we want to serve Him, we want to prove our love. If we are not careful, what has begun as a work of grace can very soon turn to striving to show our commitment.

The work of the Lord is done from a place of rest, because the victory has already been won at the cross. He wants to rest in us and invites us to rest in Him. I am in a continual battle to live from that place of rest and victory, out into life's situations. Through the scriptures, I want to lay a foundation in our hearts that will be a kind of anchor to tether us to this place of rest.

God's resting place

When Solomon had completed the temple, he dedicated it with prayer and ended by saying these words: *"And now arise, O Lord God, and go to your resting place, you and the ark of your might."*.[1]

It was an audacious prayer. He was saying in effect, *I have built this house for you, Almighty God, and now I would like you to move in! I would like you to relax and feel at home here.*

The amazing thing is that the Lord honoured Solomon's audacity. The beginning of the next chapter recounts that fire came down on the offering and the glory of the Lord filled the temple. The result was that the whole nation worshipped the Lord.[2] Where God rests, people worship! What a picture of revival.

The word 'resting place' in Hebrew is nuwach. It means to rest, to settle down, to make yourself at home, to draw breath, to relax, to quieten.

Today, we are the temples of the Lord:

What agreement has the temple of God with idols? For we are the temple of the living God; as God said,
"I will make my dwelling among them and walk among them, and I will be their God, and they shall be my people".[3]

We can pray in the same way that Solomon did. *Come*

---

1. 2 Chronicles 6:41
2. 2 Chronicles 7:1-3
3. 2 Corinthians 6:16

Lord, come to your resting place. It is a great act of faith on His part that God Himself would choose to rest in us! He dares to make His home within weak and sinful people! It is what happened on the day of Pentecost. It is still happening all over the world today. He comes to *nuwach* in us. He has faith that we will carry His glory to a waiting world. He draws us to Himself and then He comes and *nuwachs* with us.

Rest in Me

The Lord rests in us, but will we rest in Him? We know that we can be born again and filled with the Holy Spirit, and yet the glory of God does not always flow freely from our lives. Our gospel message to people is often ***Ask Jesus into your lives***. It is true that this is a wonderful part of the gospel. Jesus was Himself forsaken so that we would never have to be. When we invite Him, He always comes. He will never fail us nor forsake us. However, there is another part that He asks of us:

"Abide in me, and I in you. As the branch cannot bear fruit by itself, unless it abides in the vine, neither can you, unless you abide in me. I am the vine; you are the branches. Whoever abides in me and I in him, he it is that bears much fruit, for apart from me you can do nothing." [4]

We say, "Come into my heart, Lord Jesus", and He says

---

4. John 15:4-5

to us, *Will you also come into My heart and My life? Will you abide in Me?* What does that mean in reality? It is important to understand this secret because it is the key to great fruitfulness.

To abide, to rest, to remain in Him must be to be with Him where He is. He is everywhere, it is true, but He is also manifest in particular places at particular times. He has an amazing plan for each of us, and He goes ahead of us, drawing us to where He is, inviting us into the resting place of faith that will see Him work through our lives.

Where is He standing for you? What is He drawing you towards? He has put His own Holy Spirit in you to lead you to where He is, that place of truth:

"When the Spirit of truth comes, he will guide you into all the truth, for he will not speak on his own authority, but whatever he hears he will speak, and he will declare to you the things that are to come." [5]

This place of abiding, then, is a place of actively seeking where He is and determining to be with Him. It is a place of obedience. Jesus says again and again in His final teachings to the disciples, that the way they can show their love for Him is by keeping His commandments. When He summarised the heart of all the commandments, He said: *Love God and love*

---

5. John 16:13

your neighbour.[6]

He knows that we cannot keep these commands in our own strength. The only way we can do it is with His love in us and around us. We need to rest in Him and let Him rest in us. So He says, *"As the Father has loved me, so have I loved you. Abide in my love".*[7]

Live in My love. Enjoy My love, rest in My love, let My love shape your life. Such a simple command, but one that is profoundly hard to follow. It seems to me that human nature is anti grace. We want to prove ourselves, earn our right, demonstrate our ability. We want to live in our own 'love'.

Jesus says, Live in My love. Know that I love you! Don't make your own plans. Abide in Me and I will show you what to do, how to speak, how to be truly effective.

Learn from Me

Jesus Himself, the One who is the very Word of God, the One who formed the universe, submitted Himself entirely to His Father while He was here on earth. He did not speak or act on His own initiative:

"I have not spoken on my own authority, but the Father who sent me has himself given me a commandment -

---

6. Matthew 22:37-40

7. John 15:9

what to say and what to speak".[8]

So Jesus said to them, "Truly, truly, I say to you, the Son can do nothing of his own accord, but only what he sees the Father doing. For whatever the Father does, that the Son does likewise".[9]

He had no power to work miracles in His own right. He had emptied Himself of all His heavenly authority when He came to earth.[10] He did it so that He could be a model for us. He is flesh of our flesh.

We still get trapped by the tree of the knowledge of good and evil.[11] Knowledge in this sense is the great enemy of faith. We feel we must *know* what to do, where we are going, what the strategy is.

Are plans wrong? Should we not prepare? I think that there is a time for plans and preparations. The Lord tells us to renew our minds, not abandon them. However, the key is submission to God. Jesus did what He saw the Father doing. This is the place of rest. He did not get stressed by the demands of the crowd, nor upset when His disciples failed to understand Him. He did not care what people thought of Him.

---

8. John 12:49

9. John 5:19

10. Philippians 2:5-8

11. Genesis 2:16-17

He lived for 30 years doing nothing noteworthy. He is the resurrection and the life, yet His own earthly father died and He did nothing. He would raise others from the dead, but He *only* did what He saw His Father doing. This is true and costly submission, and true freedom.

He demonstrated this life of abiding and obedience, and then said:

"Truly, truly, I say to you, whoever believes in me will also do the works that I do; and greater works than these will he do, because I am going to the Father." [12]

His 'going to the Father' opened the Holy of Holies for us. He died to give us access to the centre of the universe, the throne of grace, the very source of Love itself. *So, He says, remain in this love. Rest into this love and let love lead you into the destiny I have prepared for you.*

Jesus is inviting us into resting from our own work. He says, *Come and be at home in Me, and I too will be at home in you.* When we are in that place of fellowship there is always fruit.

Terrifying love!

Jesus' love for us is wonderful and terrifying; *"the Father has*

---

12. John 14:12

loved me, so have I loved you".[13] God's unrelenting love for His Son led Jesus to His destiny at the cross. Love births love. Eternal love births a love so passionate, so uncompromising, so unconditional that it will go to any lengths.

✘ *Love bears all things, believes all things, hopes all things, endures all things.*[14]

This is the love with which Jesus loves us. He invites us to rest into this love. In this place of abiding, we too will be led to the cross. We too will find that we can bear all things for the sake of others who are yet to receive this glorious love. This place of rest becomes also the place of fruitfulness.

In one sense Jesus 'did' nothing when He achieved His greatest work. He submitted to His Father's will and allowed others to take Him, beat Him, and nail Him to the cross. He rested into His Father's purposes, trusting that whatever it looked like, Love would win.

So He invites us to abide in His love. This joyful, awe-full place. This place where we rest from our own work and begin to understand His heart.

Resting in Love

He teaches us to rest when He speaks in the Sermon on the Mount.

---

13. John 15:9
14. 1 Corinthians 13:7 ✟

"Therefore I tell you, do not be anxious about your life, what you will eat or what you will drink, nor about your body, what you will put on. Is not life more than food, and the body more than clothing? ... Consider the lilies of the field, how they grow: they neither toil nor spin, yet I tell you, even Solomon in all his glory was not arrayed like one of these." [15]

Could it be that Jesus was thinking of Solomon's temple when He gave this teaching? At the entrance of the temple were two pillars: Jachin (He establishes) and Boaz (in Him is strength). On top of those pillars stood two huge bronze lilies and 200 pomegranates. In front of the pillars stood a huge bronze 'sea' shaped as a lily, held up by twelve bulls.[16] This sea was not to be used for anything other than the priests to cleanse themselves in.

Lilies are a symbol of rest and trust, bulls represent work, and pomegranates fruitfulness. God has established us as His temple, and only He can enable us (strengthen us) to fulfil that role. The pillars of His temple are crowned with lilies, with rest. It is HIS WORK! *He* establishes, *He* strengthens. How often I have to come back to this after exhausting myself trying to serve Him.

As we enter into His presence in our temple, we can bathe ourselves in the 'sea' of rest. How easy it is to toil and spin, even in our attempts at prayer. Prayer can become a chore to

---

15. Mattew 6:25 & 28-29

16. 1 Kings 7:15-26

be done along with everything else in our busy lives.

He says, ***Come and bathe in my rest. Cleanse yourself from all your anxieties by resting into who I AM.*** This is a place of worship. Fruitfulness comes from rest, as the pomegranates were under the lilies. Jesus told His disciples: ***"Apart from me you can do nothing".***[17]

Perhaps this is one of the hardest things of all to believe. We seem to be able to do so much. Good intentions so easily divert us from abiding.

Interestingly the bulls are submitted under the lily in the temple design. The Lord does have work for us to do, He calls us His co-workers.[18] But true work comes out of the place of rest. In His rest we can really know His love. It is the place where we don't have anything to prove; He loves us because He loves us.

In fact the 'work' that comes out of rest often looks like failure, just as the cross looked like failure for Jesus. When we submit ourselves to Love, very often we seem to lose. Love is a seed that falls into the ground and dies. It is patient. It does not insist on its own way even when it knows that it is right. However, as the resurrection of Jesus testifies, Love never fails!

---

17. John 15:5
18. 1 Corinthians 3:9

Enjoying His love

As the Lord promised Solomon about the temple, so He commits to us: *"My eyes and my heart will always be there"*.[19]

What a love statement. *You have my eyes and my heart! I will never leave you nor forsake you. My eyes are on you. They are full of love. I see everything in you, nothing is hidden from Me, and I still love you! My heart is linked with yours. Spend time with Me, just looking into My eyes. Feel My heart beat. Let your heart beat with Mine. Let Me show you what I feel about you, and then together we can look outwards to a waiting world.*

King David, in spite of all his successes and all his responsibilities, had learnt what the most important thing was,

*One thing have I asked of the Lord,
that will I seek after:
that I may dwell in the house of the Lord
all the days of my life,
to gaze upon the beauty of the Lord
and to enquire in his temple.*[20]

In fact, I believe that it was because David made this his priority that he was able to achieve so much.

---

19. 2 Chronicles 7:16, NIV

20. Psalm 27:4

The more we gaze, the more we will see of His glory, and so the more we can see that glory manifest on earth as it is in heaven.

Miraculous rest

When Joshua crossed the Jordan river to enter the promised land, the Lord told him to instruct the priests to go ahead of the nation, carrying the ark of His presence, and stand still in the river. He said that when their feet 'rested' (Hebrew *nuwach*) in the Jordan the waters would part.[21] They carried the presence of God with their arms and shoulders. Yet that presence flowed through them as they stood in *nuwach* rest.

God's presence is still manifest in us as we rest in Him. To enter His rest, we must have faith. The priests could have been swept away by the Jordan which was in full flood. They chose to walk into the flood carrying God's presence. It was because they 'rested' in the presence of the Lord that a nation could pass by them and walk into its inheritance. Miracles and deliverance come from the place of rest.

We are born again into this rest. We know when we are saved that it is not because of our own work, it is all grace. The challenge is to continue in that rest. The Israelites at that time did not continue:

For if Joshua had given them rest, God would not have

---

21. John 3:13

spoken of another day later on. So then, there remains a Sabbath rest for the people of God, for whoever has entered God's rest has also rested from his works as God did from his. Let us therefore strive to enter that rest, so that no one may fall by the same sort of disobedience. For the word of God is living and active, sharper than any two-edged sword, piercing to the division of soul and of spirit, of joints and of marrow, and discerning the thoughts and intentions of the heart.[22]

It is in the place of rest that the Word is active! This Word is the whole character of God, that is Jesus Himself. If I will rest, He can act. It is so hard to keep re-entering that rest when everything around shouts for action. It is so tempting to think that I can help if I just do this or that. It is so easy to plan an event or even a meeting. Yet the Lord says, Strive to enter the rest. *Strive to abide in love. Strive to listen before acting. Strive to catch My heart rather than work from yours.*

In that painful place of rest, our souls are laid bare, our motives are pierced, our intentions are weighed. Yet in that place the living power of God is released and He invites us: speak with Me, walk with Me, work with Me.

Jesus luuuves you!

"Jesus luuuves you, Gail, He luuuves you so much." I tried to suppress my irritation. Of course I knew Jesus loved me, I'd

---

22. Hebrews 4:8-12

been serving Him for ten years!

I was in Egypt with a purpose in my heart. I had been working in another North African country and praying for the Lord to send Egyptian missionaries there. The church in Egypt, though repressed and persecuted, was coming into a new season of growth and life. Surely it was full of people who could go to 'my' nation and carry the gospel message. They already had the language, they understood the culture, and they were highly respected across North Africa.

I arrived at a time of fresh awakening in the group we were connected with. The 'underground' meetings were packed to the point that if someone raised their hands in worship it was doubtful that they could put them down again! They worshipped for hours, even young children of three or four years old begging to stay. People were getting saved and healed and delivered. It was incredible.

And yet I felt as though I were a spectator. I knew I was witnessing something amazing, but I just didn't feel part of it. My mind kept going to the people I had left behind. People who had no concept of how amazing the Lord really is. People with whom I had been trying to share my life and my faith.

I was expecting the Lord to speak in a powerful prophetic word so that many there would be convicted to go and share this life that they had found. He didn't, and my resentment grew. Didn't they know that they were blessed to be a blessing? How could they sing songs about loving the Lord and taking 'the land'? Surely some would be convicted to go.

I thought that if I could just share my vision with the leader that maybe he would give me the opportunity to issue a challenge. I finally got to meet him.

"Not yet, it is before the time."

How could he say that! Before the time! Didn't he realise that people were dying every day without ever having heard of Jesus?

"Jesus luuuves you, Gail!"

What has that got to do with anything? Everyone keeps telling me that. I know it already. Why aren't you listening to me? That night I wept in utter frustration. A close friend came and found me crying and gently spoke into my life:

"Do you love your work more than you love the Lord? Do you love your position more than you love the Lord?"

After that I just felt the Lord quieten me.

"It's my work, Gail. I care about those dying more than you do."

"Lay down your burden, then you can share Mine."

I was sitting on a bed just staring into nothing when suddenly my own feet came into focus. There is a very small scar on my right foot. I got it when I was a young girl trying a pair of roller skates.

"I remember when you did that."

I was overwhelmed. The Lord of the universe remembered when a little girl fell off her roller skates!

"I love you, Gail."

This time the simple words I thought I had understood came with such an intimate intensity of revelation that it was as if I had just discovered it for the very first time.

He loves me! Not just what I do for Him. He loves me! Before I even knew Him, when I was just a little girl, He loved me. I am loved.

I turned to the Song of Songs and the joyous, confident opening words of the bride echoed from my heart: ***Let him kiss me with the kisses of his mouth.***[23]

Yes Lord, I know that I am your desire, that you love me! Come and kiss me. Come and breathe into me!

---

23. Song of Songs 1:2

In God's time missionaries did go, and are still going, from Egypt into 'my' land and others. They responded to the call of their beloved, not to a need that made them feel guilty. I had found His prayer, but it was not until I got to Egypt that I began to understand something of His heart.

Chapter 3
Listening to the Beloved Warrior

Her hands were shaking as she broke the jar
Rough feet anointed with her dreams of joy.
Her prayers, her love and something she just knew,
But didn't know, yet knew she had to do
Compelled her.

She couldn't bear to look upon His face
And meet the recognition in His eyes,
The life giver, her teacher and her Lord
The One whose words had always struck a chord
Would leave her.

A voice of reason jeered, condemned the waste
Then Love spoke out, interpreted her act.
And though her heart was full she could not weep
As they had done when deep had called to deep
And freed her.
She seemed to sense the nails that soon would pierce
The feet she now anointed with her love

And He would call for iron to pierce His heart
To give the cold and hard a brand new start;
To free us.

One stone was moved to set her brother free
Another would be moved by heavenly hands
To show the world the truth of 'It is done!'
Love broken, iron pierced, yet raised with wounds
Of glory!

The Lord invites us: *Live in My love, find the place of resting from your own work and hear My living, active word that gets things done!*

Mary of Bethany had discovered the secret: it was better to listen to Jesus before trying to serve Him.

Now as they went on their way, Jesus entered a village. And a woman named Martha welcomed him into her house. And she had a sister called Mary, who sat at the Lord's feet and listened to his teaching. But Martha was distracted with much serving. And she went up to him and said, "Lord, do you not care that my sister has left me to serve alone? Tell her then to help me." But the Lord answered her, "Martha, Martha, you are anxious and troubled about many things, but one thing is necessary. Mary has chosen the good portion, which will not be taken away from her." [1]

Actually she was part of a long line of listeners: Abraham, Moses, Samuel, David, and so many more. The psalmist wrote: *For a day in your courts is better than a thousand elsewhere.*[2] A thousand days (approximately three years) of work cannot match just one day in the presence of the Lord!

We are often so time-conscious. I suspect that Martha was the same. Thirteen hungry men had arrived at their house and needed feeding. There was no time to 'waste'. How often I subconsciously feel it is better to 'do', than to spend time just sitting at Jesus' feet. I know that Mary chose the better part, but do I really believe it? My actions show me what I believe.

Jesus told Martha that she was *anxious and troubled about many things.*[3] I am sure that they were legitimate things to be anxious about. Martha was not sinning in the sense that we normally think of sin. She was doing something good. She was being hospitable. She was busy with many things, but it was keeping her from the 'one thing' that was needful at that time.

The word *'anxious'* in Greek actually has the same root as the good *'portion'* or thing that Mary had found. It is to do with being distracted, divided into parts or portions. Martha

---

1. Luke 10:38-42
2. Psalm 84:10
3. Luke 10:41

was in many *'portions'*, Mary had just one *'portion'*.

The person who is single-minded about seeking the Lord will always be the one who is successful. Anxiety directly attacks our capacity to listen to Him. Martha's mind was full of noise; what did she have in the house? How could she get a good meal in front of them? Where was that sister of hers?

Not only was Martha affected herself, but she was in danger of blocking her sister's fellowship with Jesus. Anxiety is an affliction common to us all. We need to recognise it for what it is, rather than naming it 'service for God' or some other 'holy' thing. The fruit of anxiety is that we feel overburdened, and resentful. We find ourselves isolated because no one wants to come under the same burden we are carrying. If we don't deal with it, others too can be tainted and distracted by us.

Once it is named, we can choose to turn from it.

Jesus tells us, *"Do not be anxious about your life"*.[4] Don't be distracted from the one thing that is important, to do the many things that seem to need doing.

> *"But seek first the kingdom of God and his righteousness, and all these things will be added to you."* [5]

---

4. Matthew 6:25

5. Matthew 6:33

That is what Mary was doing. Life is busy, it is full of demands, yet we have the choice to be different to those around us who run after what to eat, to drink, to wear.

Listening is humbling

To choose to listen before acting is in effect to say, *You know better than I do.* Of course, we would all agree that is true when it comes to Almighty God. However, since humankind ate that fruit of the tree of the knowledge there is something deep within us that just hates to be in a place of helplessness. We want to know, to understand, to be in control.

As we wait for Jesus to speak, we realise our own lack. We see that we have nothing without Him. It cuts across our pride. Unless He speaks we have nothing to say; unless He shows us what to do, we are utterly useless.

Yet, if we will persevere in that place of helplessness, we will find an incredible freedom. John the Baptist found that place and knew overflowing joy because of it. He said, *"A person cannot receive even one thing unless it is given him from heaven".*[6]

In that place he could joyfully recognise his role in the kingdom of God. He was free from jealousy, free from burdens, free simply to rejoice in what Jesus was doing. It

---

6. John 3:27

wasn't his work, but it belonged to the Lord.

When we come to listen (which is the most important component of prayer), we need to quieten our thoughts, anxieties and plans. Sometimes this seems almost impossible to do. I find it helps me to read Scripture aloud slowly, trying to drink in the meaning. In doing that, perspective comes and my inner emotional storms gradually die down.

It seems as if our souls and spirits are only so big. If they are full of unrest, there is no space to receive God's word. We need to empty out the anxiety and all that goes with it to create space inside for Him to speak.

I imagine that Jesus' gaze upon Mary, as she sat at His feet to listen, was one of great tenderness. He still longs for our company! He invites us to enjoy His presence. We can come, not demanding anything, simply loving Him. If we put ourselves, like Mary, in a place of listening, then He can speak when He wants to. Good friends do not always need to be speaking. It's great just to sit quietly and meditate on how wonderful He is.

Meditation

Meditation is a tremendous gift to God's people. Satan has tried to hijack it. Most of us would automatically think of eastern religions when we think of meditation. Generally those religions and disciplines teach people to 'empty themselves'. Biblical meditation is exactly the opposite: it invites us to fill ourselves with God's words. Jesus says, *"If you abide in me, and my words abide in you, ask whatever you wish, and it will be done for you".*[7] Paul tells us: *Let the word of Christ dwell in you richly.*[8]

The Bible speaks a lot about meditating on the word of God. Joshua was told that if he would meditate it would help him to obey God's word, and he would be successful in whatever he did. David in his psalms continually speaks of meditating on God's word.[9]

There are several words in Scripture that are translated as meditate, yet they all have the same sense: *to muse, to commune, to murmur, to imagine, to pour forth thoughts.*

In fact if you think about it, we all meditate every day. Our only choice is: what do we want to meditate on? A lot of anxiety and stress are brought on because we meditate on the wrong thing.

It doesn't take a genius to realise that if people meditate on God's word, they are likely to hear Him. Satan knows that too and I believe that is why he has tried to contaminate this precious means of blessing. Today we cannot sit physically at the feet of Jesus, but if we will meditate on Him and His word,

---

7. John 15:7

8. Colossians 3:16

9. Joshua 1:8; Psalms 1:1-3; 48:9; 77:12; 119:15, 23, 48, 78, 97, 99, 148; 143:5; 145:5

we take that position spiritually.

Roots of meditation

When we want to understand the root of something in Scripture, it is often good to go back to the first time it is mentioned. The first person who is mentioned in the Bible as meditating is Isaac. He meditated in the fields in the evening as he waited for his bride.[10] As he was meditating, he looked up and saw her coming.

If we look at the story we see that Abraham, a type of the Father, had sent his servant, a type of the Holy Spirit, to search for a bride of the same blood as his son Isaac, who was himself a type of Christ. Isaac trusted his father and was anticipating with joy the arrival of his bride.

Jesus is longing for His bride. He is meditating on us, waiting and watching for us. He has asked the Father, who has sent the Holy Spirit to search in every tribe and nation for a bride of His royal blood. A cleansed and pure bride who will love Him only. Are we longing as He is? Are we meditating on our Beloved Warrior?

How do we meditate?

So how do we meditate? It seems to me there are three main ways of reading the Bible; devotional reading is by far the most common. This is when we read a passage, possibly

---

10. Genesis 24:63

with study notes, and see if something jumps out at us. The second way is to study the Bible; to delve into a book or a theme or a character in Scripture. This is vital to our grasping the whole message of the *logos* word of God. The third way is to meditate on a few words of Scripture. Meditating and study belong together.

When we meditate, it is like chewing on the word of God. If we try to bite off too much, we cannot enjoy it. We get a kind of spiritual indigestion. God's word is so powerful that to even begin to draw some of the meaning and life from it we must take small 'mouthfuls' and chew it well. We can fool ourselves into thinking that we know God's word, but unless we are daily chewing on it, digesting it, and applying it personally, it is only head knowledge.

So to meditate we take a small part of God's word, maybe a verse, or even just a few words. It may have been something that 'jumped out' at us from our morning reading, or we may choose a particular book of the Bible to meditate through.

We ponder those living active words. As we muse on them, we can start to commune with the Lord by asking questions: *What are you saying to me from these words today? How should they change my life today?*

Often when we look at a passage, we remember a good sermon we have heard, or maybe something that the Lord said to us before about it. If we want to get something new, it is best to put those things to one side for the time being.

The word of God is so amazing that if we will give ourselves to meditate on it, we will continually discover new ways in which the Lord is speaking to us.

Meditation is to do with getting things from our heads to our hearts. It is an exercise of the spirit rather than the mind. It is not to do with how well we know the Scriptures, though of course it is important to get to know them and study them. Meditation allows the newest believer to feed on God's word themselves.

Meditating on one word - **Father** - has profoundly affected my life. Coming to know God as Father. Responding to Him as my Father. Allowing Him to respond to me as my Father. God of the universe and *my Father!*

Meditation changes the our of Scripture to the *my*. The apostle Paul spoke of *my* gospel.[11] He wasn't being exclusive, but he was celebrating personal revelation that had forever changed him. He must have spent time meditating on Isaiah 49:6:

"It is too light a thing that you should be my servant
to raise up the tribes of Jacob
and to bring back the preserved of Israel;
I will make you as a light for the nations,
that my salvation may reach to the end of the earth."

---

11. Romans 2:16; 16:25; 2 Timonthy 2:8

That promise is written to the nation of Israel and the you is plural. However, when Paul is giving his testimony in Acts 13:47, it has become a singular promise to him personally. God had spoken it to him, and nothing would ever be the same again. It transformed his whole life and guided his ministry.

Being taught to meditate has been one of the greatest gifts I have ever received. Rowland Evans, the leader of the mission movement I joined, trained us in almost 'army style'. To begin with, he got us to meditate our way through one verse of Scripture word by word: *"If you ask me anything in my name, I will do it"*.[12]

Each day at 8am, a group of us would sit on the floor in his tiny office while he listened to our feedback of what the Lord had said to us from the word *'if'* (or whatever it happened to be that day).

I have to say, I struggled. It took me a while to get it. Rowland would continually say to us, **"Don't manufacture something, just be real. Listen to what God is dropping into your spirit".**

Gradually things began to 'click'. Most of us are not used to exercising our spirits. I certainly wasn't. However, suddenly that little word *if* began to open up a whole world of potential for me. The Lord was inviting me to ask. He wanted to know

---

12. John 14:14

my thoughts. I was important to Him.

To help us to meditate through the day, Rowland would ask us to stop at the start of every hour and discipline ourselves to remember the Scripture on which we were meditating and, for a few minutes, just to chew on it again.

In time, I found that I could meditate on a Scripture in my heart while I was doing something else. My work didn't need to disturb my communion with the Lord. Just as we can subconsciously worry about something, so in a positive way we can subconsciously meditate.

To me this wonderful gift has been my mainstay of hearing the Lord. As I chew on His word, He reveals Himself.

Revelation

You cannot build a theology on meditation. It is personal revelation. Yet that revelation will lead us into intimacy with the One who is breathing His word into us. Jesus himself said, ***"Man shall not live by bread alone, but by every word that comes from the mouth of God".***[13]

There are two words in Greek that are both translated 'word' in English: ***logos*** and ***rhema***. ***Logos*** speaks of the whole word of God, the Bible. It is also the name for Jesus Himself:

---

13. Mattew 4:4

In the beginning was the Word (logos), and the Word (logos) was with God, and the Word (logos) was God.[14]

Logos is a wonderful concept. It means the reason, the purpose, the Word. We must know the **Logos**, the person of Jesus and His wonderful gift to us, the Bible.

Rhema literally means spoken word (connected with breathing out), and it is this of which Jesus speaks when He says we live by the words that come from the mouth of God.

The Bible exhorts us to *live by faith* and then tells us, *So faith comes from hearing, and hearing through the word (rhema) of Christ.*[15]

When we study God's word we are studying the *logos.* Context is vital, overview is important. However, when we meditate we are searching for God's *rhema*. It will never conflict with the logos, but it can happen that the Holy Spirit may take a word out of its original context and apply it to our particular situation.

Meditation is a wonderful way of feeding on God's word and opening ourselves to hear His voice. Our Beloved Warrior has many things He wants to whisper into our hearts.

---

14. John 1:1
15. Romans 10:17

Our place prepared

Mary of Bethany was one who had learnt to meditate on the *rhema* words that Jesus spoke. It was because of this that she knew that Jesus had prepared a place for her at His feet. Each time we see her in the gospels, that is where she is. When we determine to listen for whatever Jesus says, we become aware of the place that He has prepared for us, a place of intimacy where we can come to Him, even in the midst of the battle.

We see Mary of Bethany three times in the Scriptures. The first time listening at Jesus' feet[16], the second falling prostrate in grief at His feet[17], and the third anointing His feet[18]. In devotion, in grief and in worship her place was prepared. She knew that she could come, and would not be turned away.

Disappointment

One of the things that often blocks us from hearing what the Lord is whispering to us is that we have already made up our minds what the answer should be. That was the situation in which Mary and Martha found themselves when their brother was ill. They immediately sent for Jesus and had no doubt that He would come and heal Lazarus. They waited and waited, knowing that He loved them and would not let them down. Yet He didn't come, at least not until it was too late.

---

16. Luke 10:39
17. John 11:32
18. John 12:3

Have you been in that place? It seems like a place of faith. You know the Lord, you know His promises. You believe that He will answer you. You have waited in faith, and then the unspeakable has happened. The answer didn't come. All you are left with is deep disappointment and confusion.

The sisters had agreed together on what Jesus should have done. If you read the account in John 11, Mary and Martha say exactly the same thing when they meet Jesus: **"Lord, if you had been here, my brother would not have died".**[19]

What they were really saying was: **You should have been here. You should have healed him. Why didn't you come?** They had talked together in their grief and disappointment, and their conclusion was that Jesus had got it wrong.

We probably wouldn't consciously allow ourselves to think in those terms, but how often have we in effect blamed God when we think we can see the way that He should have answered a certain situation?

For the sisters and for us, what we think 'should have' happened can potentially be the block to us participating in what Jesus actually wants to do. Anger, despair or bitterness can obstruct our relationship with Jesus.

What saved Mary and Martha is the same thing that can save us. They went out to meet Jesus when He came. Even

---

19. John 11:21 & 32

though they blamed Him, they still went to Him. They spoke with Him, they listened to what He had to say.

It is so beautiful to see how Jesus deals with each of them individually. They are such different people, and Jesus respects that.

Martha was the thinker and the doer. She was also a woman of faith. Even in her grief and confusion she professed: *"But even now I know that whatever you ask from God, God will give you"*.[20]

She was longing to understand Jesus, so He opened her mind to begin to grapple with the fact that although she knew truths, for example that her brother would rise again on the last day, she was actually standing in front of the One who is the Truth. He spoke real reality to her - *"I am the resurrection and the life"*[21] - and it was too big for her mind to contain.

Martha saw that she had to let go of her desire to be in control of everything. She could not put this in order or tidy it away. This truth was beyond understanding, it could only be grasped by faith. So she declared who she knew He was, that He was God, and as such, what He said must be true. In doing that she came to a place of peace. *"Yes, Lord; I believe that you are the Christ, the Son of God, who is coming into the*

---

20. John 11:22
21. John 11:25

world".[22]

Jesus allowed her to speak out her faith.

Jesus had gently led her to a resting place of faith in the midst of her grief before her circumstances changed.

Mary was quite different. Perhaps she was even more heartbroken than her sister. She had a special place of intimacy with Jesus, and yet He had ignored her urgent plea. She was not interested in understanding, what was important to her was what came from the heart.

She was too hurt to go out with her sister and meet Jesus, but when she heard that He was asking for her she ran to Him. Love, once kindled, is the flame that will draw us as we allow Him to woo us through the heartbreak to the healing.

The only words she could get out were the ones that she and her sister had agreed together: **"Lord, if you had been here, my brother would not have died".**[23]

She loved Him. She knew He loved her. Why had He let his happen? All she could do was weep. Jesus didn't even try to speak with her. He spoke to those who had come with her, asking where Lazarus' body was, but He knew that for Mary words would be meaningless. So He opened His heart to her in the only way that she could understand; He wept.[24]

---

22. John 11:27
23. John 11:21 & 32
24. John 11:35

The Scripture speaks of Jesus being 'deeply moved' in His spirit[25], which in the Greek means angry, indignant. These are not emotions that we normally associate with tears. However, there were two different things going on in Jesus at the same time. The anger was His reaction as the Son of God to the spirit of death that had taken his friend Lazarus. His tears of compassion were His response as the Son of Man to this woman who had opened her heart to Him.

When we listen to our beloved, sometimes we hear Him weeping with us in our brokenness. Sometimes He is inviting us to weep with Him in compassion that will move us to action for others in their suffering. At other times still He is snorting indignantly as He sees the enemy trying to steal life. At times like that our Beloved Warrior challenges us: *"Did I not tell you that if you believed you would see the glory of God?"* [26] and invites us to roll away the stone and speak with Him declaring who He is: the resurrection and the life!

Deep calls to deep

The final time we see Mary of Bethany she is anointing Jesus' feet. She must of course have been overwhelmed when Jesus raised her brother from the dead. Yet it seems to me that it was more than simple thankfulness that prompted her. Mary was a listener. She listened with all of her heart. Perhaps the most precious gift that a believer can seek is the gift of truly listening.

---

25. John 11:33
26. John 11:40

As we listen, we begin to see. John, the beloved disciple, was another listener. He found his place with Jesus, resting on His breast.[27] Such an intimate place; in fact that was the very place that Jesus had with His Father.[28] He rested on His breast.

When Jesus gave John the revelation on the Island of Patmos, John said, Then I turned to **see** the voice that was speaking to me, and on turning I **saw**...[29]

He goes on to describe the Lord in all His glory. John saw so much because he first listened. Listening to Jesus always leads to revelation! Mary too saw something because she was listening. Maybe her mind did not grasp what was being revealed, but her spirit did, and she responded. She must have seen something of what her Lord was going to suffer. It was six days before the Passover that Jesus visited their house.

Instinctively she followed her heart. The deep longing in Jesus for someone to understand Him, someone to stand with Him on His journey to the cross, reached into her depths and stirred her to action. Deep was calling to deep. In some mysterious way, Mary was having a revelation of Jesus as the bridegroom.

---

27. John 13:25
28. John 1:18
29. Revelation 1:12, emphasis added

Nard, or spikenard, is a precious perfume made from the crushing of blossoms. Jewish girls, who were able to afford such a treasure, would often keep it to anoint their wedding bed. Mary was not just anointing Jesus with expensive perfume, she was pouring her dreams, her longings at His feet. In doing so she anointed Him for burial and became the only person who encouraged and ministered to Him on the way to the cross.

She also fulfilled prophecy. The bride in the Song of Solomon anointed her King with nard. The one who is greater than Solomon was before Mary reclining (as was the custom in the Middle East) to eat on his couch.

While the king was on his couch, my nard gave forth its fragrance.[30]

It was in the heart of the Father that His Son should receive this anointing. The crushed flowers of the nard spoke of the crushing of the rose of Sharon, the King of shalom. Mary had learnt to listen to the deep things of God and so responded to what she didn't fully understand. Understanding didn't matter, love did.

Mary's offering was outrageous in the eyes of some. It was not just what she gave - the valuable nard which was worth a year's wages poured out in a moment - but the way she gave it... pouring it not just on Jesus' head, but on His feet and then wiping it in with her own hair!

---

30. Song of solomon 1:12

This was unseemly behaviour to say the least, but Mary didn't care. Hair in the Bible is always a sign of devotion. Just think about the story of Samson. He was chosen from birth to be a Nazarite. A Nazarite was someone who was set apart for God. Part of the vows that he or she made were to never cut their hair. Hair is the 'crown' of our physical body (a woman's crowning glory as spoken of by Paul in 1 Corinthians 11:15).

Mary was displaying her utter devotion to Jesus. She could do it because she had learnt to listen with her heart to the unspoken longings of God.

In this act of love Mary did not only bless Jesus, but became a blessing to every nation. Jesus said, **"And truly, I say to you, wherever the gospel is proclaimed in the whole world, what she has done will be told in memory of her"**.[31]

I believe it is always true that when we listen and respond to Jesus, we become what He promised to our father Abraham: a blessing to the nations.

Rhythm

As I write I am struggling with a heart complaint that has recently been diagnosed: atrial fibrillation. It means that my heart is beating irregularly. It has left me tired and a little breathless and dizzy. I can only type for a few minutes at a time, and frequently have to go and lie on the couch to

---

31. Mark 14:9

counter the dizzy spells.

However, in the few weeks since I have had these symptoms I have felt the Lord very close. I know He can heal me in an instant, and I don't believe He has brought this upon me; after all, He is the Lord of life. It is Satan who comes to steal and kill and destroy. Yet I sense Him using this time and reminding me of a week I spent with Him on a personal retreat ten years ago.

I would like to say that I regularly have such retreats. It has always been my intention. However, much as I aspire to Mary's part, I often find myself emulating Martha. I am a broken 'doer' who continually has to find her way back to her place at the feet of Jesus.

On that retreat I felt the Lord inviting me to come with Him into the darkness. A strange invitation, and yet I came to realise that the Holy of Holies was a place of complete darkness. The Holy Place had the lamp stand, and the outer courts were full of natural light, but the only light in the Holy of Holies must have come from heaven. Earthly light enables us to measure the passing of time. I am so time-oriented! Heaven's light releases us to touch eternity.

In my mind I had thought that my retreat would be a time when I could wait on the Lord for His word. I had many ministry appointments scheduled; I also had decisions to make regarding the work I was leading. However, as I waited in the darkness there was no word, only presence.

Time hung very heavily for me at the beginning. I knew I needed to slow my inner being. I was aware of the minutes passing. I kept going into Scripture trying to find what the Lord was saying to me. I pulled out meaning, but remained unsatisfied.

In the beginning, God created the heavens and the earth. The earth was without form and void, and darkness was over the face of the deep. And the Spirit of God was hovering over the face of the waters.[32]

I realised that the Lord was there in the empty and formless darkness as much as He was when He spoke the world into being. He was before the beginning, and He will be after the end. I cannot conform Him to space and time. He chooses to humbly come into the limits of time and space to communicate with me.

I was staying in a cottage, miles from anywhere, in west Wales. There was no ambient light, and when the October nights drew in I found peace just sitting in the darkness, and enjoying the Lord. I felt His presence hovering over my own emptiness and formlessness. I began to realise that He did not need words to communicate. I was being loved, being held, being treasured.

---

32. Genesis 1:1-2

It was a time beyond description. A time when I began to understand what David meant when he said that deep calls to deep.[33] With a surge of joy, I also realised that I was loving Him. Words seemed irrelevant, but my heart was overflowing with something beyond gratitude. Something that I knew I had received so that I could give. I realised that I was worshipping Him in Spirit and truth.

A few months before that retreat I had lost my father. He died in hospital of a superbug. In the darkness I felt my heavenly Father hold me close to His chest, and put my ear against His heart. I had often laid that way as a little girl in my earthly father's arms.

As I lay there, I could sense His heartbeat. I knew I was being held in the centre of everything. All I needed to do was to hear His heart and allow my heart to beat in time with His.

I felt that something had shifted. Questions I had come with had found their answer. I didn't know what the answer was, but I knew it was there for me to find when I left. I felt that my Father was moving circumstances around me to conform to His purposes. Our hearts were beating as one because I was recognising the incredible truth: my Creator and I are family!

During the following months I stood amazed at how the Lord worked among us and brought agreement among

---

33. Psalm 42:7

believers. I also found that I was speaking out of an overflow of life in me, often without consciously preparing. I was right, something had shifted; it was me. I had learned for a while to stand into the kingdom of heaven, into the eternal realm. I discovered that as I worship, the Lord is at work.

I write this now with an aching longing. My heart condition seems to me a picture of where I am at the moment. I have been told that my heart is beating too fast and that it has too many electrical impulses coming into it, so it is being pulled in many different directions.

"Martha, Martha, you are anxious and troubled about many things, but one thing is necessary." [34]

What a hard but infinitely precious lesson to learn. How kind is the Lord that He does not tire of bringing me back again and again to that one necessary thing.

---

34. Luke 10:41-42

Chapter 4
Woshipping the Beloved Warrior

Can I really come here every day?
This place beyond songs.
This place where the core of me belongs.

Here I am known
Here I know.

Here I breathe deeply
Here I feel Your breath.

This is a place of love,
Darkness protects,
Silence embraces,
Undemanding yet inviting.

Here we laugh
Here shalom finds me again.

Can I really come here every day?

Amazing. We really can come! In the midst of everyday life we can be with our beloved in the kingdom of heaven. We can stand into the mystery that is the throne room of God.

I have come to realise that as I set my heart to come to Him, as I let go of my own agenda, laying down the need for answers, I find that I am worshipping Him.

Worship is enjoying God. It is demonstrating to Him that He is our beloved, that there is no one we would rather be with. Worship is gazing on His face and allowing Him to gaze upon us. It is the complete giving of ourselves in loving response to who God is or, as the apostle Paul put it, ***offering our bodies as a living sacrifice.***[1]

When we worship we find ourselves in love. It is a discovery that believers have made throughout the millennia. Perhaps nowhere is it better expressed than in the passionate love song that is at the very centre of our Bibles, the Song of Songs. The song of a maiden to her King and her lover, and His song to her. It is a wonderful allegory of how the King of kings loves us, and longs for our love too.

The two main characters are King Solomon and the Shulamite. Both names have their root in the Hebrew word shalom. This word means much more than peace; it speaks of wholeness, complete restoration to what is perfect. King Solomon gained peace in his lifetime but lost a lasting

---

1. Romans 12:1, NIV

inheritance through self-indulgence. The Prince of Peace, Jesus, has completely restored *shalom* to all who will receive it by His selfless love.

This song is the journey of a bride to discover that she is created to be of the same essence (*shalom*) as her lover, and that her whole being is in harmony when she is united with Him.

The maiden expresses her longing for her lover's kiss. In perfect assurance that He desires her, she invites Him, **Let him kiss me.**[2]

The rabbis teach that this kiss from the Lord is given as He breathes His word into us. **Kiss** in Hebrew is nasaq. It also means to equip, or to arm a warrior. Our Beloved Warrior calls us to be like Him. He arms us with His words of love. He gives us weapons through our intimacy with Him. Jesus calls us to a strange violence that will turn this world upside down. And our weapon is love.

The Song of Songs traces the journey of the bride as she learns to truly worship her beloved. She starts as a newborn, yet still very self-serving, believer. However, she matures to be the helpmeet who will run with her beloved on the mountains, overcoming every obstacle, to see others come into His love.

The Song sees her learning to understand the heart of her

---

2. Song of Songs 1:2

bridegroom rather than fixing her eyes on herself. To go into detail about this needs a book in its own right. In this chapter I would just like to draw a few lessons from it as we follow the bride's journey.

Sin does not lessen God's love for us

One of the things that keeps us from the presence of the Lord is a sense of unworthiness. Our head knows that we are forgiven and cleansed by His blood, but so often our hearts betray us. It is easy to fix our eyes on our own weaknesses. Let's learn to sing with the bride, I am very dark, but lovely.[3] Our sin does not stop Jesus from loving us!

But God shows his love for us in that **while we were still sinners**, Christ died for us.[4]

When condemnation threatens to overwhelm us, we can declare: yes we are dark, darkened by the sun of this world, darkened by our own deeds, and what others have inflicted on us,[5] but nonetheless, we are lovely in God's eyes!

I am sure that it hardly needs saying that the darkness spoken of here is nothing to do with the natural wonder of the rich array of skin tones that the Lord has created. It is to do with the circumstances in which we find ourselves, created

---

3. Song of Songs 1:5

4. Romans 5:8, emphasis added

5. Song of Songs 1:6

by the sin of others, and by our own sin.

We are so lovely to Him, that He is always longing to 'kiss' us. He waits for our invitation. Are we hungry for His touch, His word? Are we desperate for Him? There is a holy confidence that comes as we allow His words of love to wash over us.

The bridegroom in the song calls His dark and immature bride *most beautiful of women.*[6] He does not dwell on our failings, but always looks upon us as we are created to be.

The great worshipping warrior, King David understood this. Listen to him in Psalm 103,

He does not deal with us according to our sins,
nor repay us according to our iniquities.
For as high as the heavens are above the earth,
so great is his steadfast love towards those who fear him.[7]

What David saw in shadows, we now know in the reality of the wonder of the cross of Jesus. The veil is torn! The divide between heaven and earth has been forever removed. We are forgiven, we are accepted, we are loved! This revelation releases us to truly worship our King.

In love, Jesus has laid out a banquet for us in the kingdom

---

6. Song of Songs 1:8, NIV

7. Psalm 103:10-11

of heaven. He invites us to sit with Him and eat.

> *He brought me to the banqueting house,*
> *and his banner over me was love.*[8]

We have done nothing to deserve it, He has done all the work. Our part is simply to believe and feast with Him. As we revel in His love, we find that we cannot contain it; we have to allow it to overflow to others. So He invites us to arise and follow Him into the unknown.

Worship will lead us to faith

> *My beloved speaks and says to me:*
> *"Arise, my love, my beautiful one,*
> *and come away".*[9]

The kingdom of heaven is near, it is real, we experience it. As we are worshipping the Lord it feels as if we can, and will, do anything He asks. Yet, when the crunch comes, we often respond as the bride does here. She hides, she becomes silent. The reality of what He is asking hits her. The world around tells her, **Be careful, be wise**. The fruit of the tree of the knowledge of good and evil again becomes very desirable. It is good to judge for herself, to plan, to take stock. Very soon she finds herself conforming to this world rather than being transformed by the renewing of her mind, which is the fruit of

---

8. Song of Song 2:4

9. Song of Songs 2:10

true worship.[10]

So He must plead with her:

"O my dove, in the clefts of the rock,
in the crannies of the cliff,
let me see your face,
let me hear your voice,
for your voice is sweet,
and your face is lovely.
Catch the foxes for us,
the little foxes
that spoil the vineyards,
for our vineyards are in blossom".[11]

Little foxes are, more often than not, the things that spoil our intimacy with Jesus. It is seldom the big sins or dangers, but those niggling little habits or fears; the small offences we hold on to; the seemingly unanswered prayer that festers. Little foxes running in a blossoming vineyard would have the ability to knock blossoms off. The fewer the blossoms, the less the fruit. Jesus will never love us any less when we refuse and disobey Him, but our own fruitfulness is compromised.

We can still worship Him in this state, and incredibly He still lovingly receives our worship. However, as we see from the bride's declaration of love, it is 'self'-oriented:

10. Romans 12:1-2

11. Songs of Songs 2:14-15

My beloved is mine, and I am his.[12]

She is first interested in her own satisfaction, that she will be blessed. By the end of the song this is completely reversed:

*I am my beloved's,
and his desire is for me.*[13]

There is not even a mention of self-gratification, only that her beloved may be satisfied. And yet in that place she is more blessed, fulfilled and fruitful than at any other time.

What motivates us to worship? Is it because we know that as we come to Him we will find peace, we will be blessed? Of course Jesus wants to bless us, but how it must hurt His heart sometimes to listen to the selfishness of our prayers, and receive our self-serving worship. Yet still He does receive it! He does not condemn, but loves us into maturity if we will allow Him to.

The bride calls out for her lover from the place of her own comfort:

*On my bed by night
I sought him whom my soul loves;
I sought him, but found him not.*[14]

---
12. Song of Songs 2:16
13. Song of Songs 7:10
14. Song of Songs 3:1

What a picture of us when we are in our 'bless me' mentality. It is a token of His love that He will not always satisfy our selfishness. Of course He is with us, but we cannot feel His presence because we are demanding, *Come to me, be with me, leave Your purposes and come and bless what I am doing.*

Jesus graciously comes into our lives by the power of His Spirit, but He longs for us to live in Him, to work with Him and be where He is. In this chapter of the song, when the bride leaves her bed to look for Him, she quickly finds Him. His withholding the manifestation of His presence draws her out. Yet, as soon as she finds Him she brings Him back to the comfort of her mother's house.[15]

What grace Jesus shows us! Even in our selfish worship, He is willing to reveal His heart. To His beloved who was not willing to go with Him into a world of lost people, He shows His wedding procession. He reveals His majesty and gives her a glimpse of some of His *mighty men*, His warriors.[16] There are so many more who are with us than against us. He is wooing His bride out of her fear, into the reality of who He is: the Lord of hosts, the King!

He sings words of tender, undeserved love over us:

You are altogether beautiful, my love;

---

15. Song of Songs 3:4
16. Song of Songs 3:6-11

there is no flaw in you.[17]

Jesus always speaks the truth, but how can this be true? These are words to a bride who is far from perfect.

Jesus looked at a volatile fisherman, Simon, and called him Peter, the rock. He spoke the truth of who Simon really was, not who He knew him to be at that time. The Lord saw the manipulator Jacob, and wrestled with him. He brought him to a point of separation from all that had held him captive. Jacob left his family and all he owned the other side of the Jabbok River (Jabbok means 'emptying'). It was then that the Lord could face him with his true identity: Israel, a prince with God, through whom He would build a nation.

Mary Magdalene, from whom Jesus cast seven demons, was not called after her father or husband as would have been usual for the time and culture in which she lived. Could it be that Jesus gave her that name Magdalene - which means 'tower' - because He saw a true strength in her? She was the one to whom He entrusted His first appearance as the resurrected Lord.

Our beloved looks at us, in all our struggle and weakness and doubt and says, You are altogether beautiful. It is His faith in us that releases us into a place of faith!

---

17. Song of Songs 4:7

Worship will lead us to challenge and suffering

From this place of faith we can declare with the bride:

*Awake, O north wind,
and come, O south wind!
Blow upon my garden,
let its spices flow.*[18]

How many times when we are lost in worship do we declare, *I will do anything, I love you, I trust you?* We invite whatever winds the Holy Spirit will blow upon us, be they the gentle south wind or the cold north wind.

Yet the bride, so like us, finds that when her beloved knocks on her door and disturbs her sleep, she is full of excuses:

*I had put off my garment;
how could I put it on?
I had bathed my feet;
how could I soil them?*[19]

How patient and gentle is our bridegroom. He sees beyond our selfishness to the deep longing within us. He knows that we really do love Him, and that even though our

---

18. Song of Songs 4:16
19. Song of Songs 5:3

flesh is so weak, our spirit is still willing.[20]

I so easily lose perspective. I am worshipping one minute, and the next I am thinking about dinner. If you are like me, just know that Jesus does not condemn us. He understands us and He, like the lover in the Song of Songs, keeps reaching out to us, wooing us, loving us. Our part is to realise our mistakes and turn again towards Him. I find worship a continual lesson in repentance!

Chapter 5 of the Song of Songs gives us an insight into the mystery of suffering as we show our love to Him by our obedience. Have you had that experience? You have responded to the voice of the Lord. You have followed Him out into the darkness, but then it seems He has disappeared. You have made sacrifices because you were sure He was calling you, but everything goes wrong. You end up beaten and bruised inside.

I am so grateful for the lesson we have in the Song of Songs. The bride has now learnt to take her eyes off herself in this situation. When she is suffering, she chooses to worship.

> *The watchmen found me*
> *as they went about in the city;*
> *they beat me, they bruised me,*
> *they took away my veil,*
> *those watchmen of the walls.*
> *I adjure you, O daughters of Jerusalem,*

---

20. Matthew 26:41

if you find my beloved,
that you tell him
I am sick with love.[21]

This lovesickness dominates her heart, so that the suffering of this world becomes irrelevant. Paul put it like this:

So we do not lose heart. Though our outer self is wasting away, our inner self is being renewed day by day. For this light momentary affliction is preparing for us an eternal weight of glory beyond all comparison, as we look not to the things that are seen but to the things that are unseen. For the things that are seen are transient, but the things that are unseen are eternal.[22]

This is a turning point for the bride. Though she does not realise it, her worship through the suffering has impacted others. People come and ask her why her beloved is better than any other.[23] The following verses are a release of sweet, unselfish worship. She pours out her adoration to the one she loves. She is oblivious to others, but surely they are challenged and drawn. True worship affects the spiritual atmosphere and, in turn, the people who witness it.

The bride is truly looking beyond this world into the unseen. It seems that the Lord allows us to suffer, even seeming to withdraw His presence at times, so that we discover

---

21. Song of Songs 5:7-8
22. 2 Corinthians 4:16-18
23. Song of Songs 5:9

just how much we love Him. He too wants to be pursued.

Suffering will purify us if we allow it to wean us from the things of this world. As this happens others will see our faith and be drawn to our beloved.

Worship is practising His presence

My beloved has gone down to his garden
to the beds of spices,
to graze in the gardens
and to gather lilies.
I am my beloved's and my beloved is mine;
he grazes among the lilies.[24]

After choosing to worship through her ordeal, the bride suddenly becomes aware that her beloved had never left her. She is His garden, and He has been in her all along. Her worship is now centred on Him, she belongs to Him; that is her joy. She now knows, through her experience, that He will never leave her! Her declaration of love is reversed, putting His interests first: *I am my beloved's and my beloved is mine.*

Jesus, in His passionate prayer of John 17, poured His heart out to His Father in the same way, putting the bride's interests first. This is true love. The culmination of that prayer is this:

---

24. Song of Songs 6:2-3

*"I made known to them your name, and I will continue to make it known, that the love with which you have loved me may be in them, and **I in them**".*[25]

It was Jesus' consuming passion that His bride would enter into the same love He enjoys with the Father, and that He would be able to be *in* us, expressing that love. He held back from us nothing of Himself or what He has. His longing began to find an answer on the day of Pentecost, through the power of the Holy Spirit, and is still finding answer in us today.

The Song of Songs prophetically foresees this mystery. The bridegroom is in the bride, browsing in her garden. He is at home. They are one flesh, one spirit, and they will in the end be one in nature.

As the bride reaches this level of maturity, she is able to realise that whatever her emotions and experiences tell her, her Lord will never desert her. When the bridegroom sees this faith His heart overflows, and He proclaims that His bride is not only full of beauty, but full of strength!

You are beautiful as Tirzah, my love,
lovely as Jerusalem,
awesome as an army with banners.[26]

The more she worships, the more she becomes like the

---
25. John 17:26, emphasis added

26. Song of Songs 6:4, emphasis added

one she is worshipping. It is a principle in Scripture that we become like that we worship.

*They followed worthless idols
and became worthless themselves.*[27]

Beloved, we are God's children now, and what we will be has not yet appeared; but we know that when he appears we shall be like him, because we shall see him as he is.[28]

Our God is a mighty warrior. His weapon is love. He is calling His warrior bride to His side. As we choose to worship when we are in pain, when we don't understand, when we cannot feel His presence, so we discover that His power is made perfect in our weakness.[29] We too become beloved warriors.

How precious this walk of faith is to Jesus. His heart is overwhelmed by our decision to love Him for who He is, not for what He can give us.

*Turn away your eyes from me,
for they overwhelm me.*[30]

---

27. Jeremiah 2:5, NIV
28. 1 John 3:2
29. 2 Corinthians 12:9
30. Song of Songs 6:5

Worship leads to action

Come, my beloved,
let us go out into the fields
and lodge in the villages;
let us go out early to the vineyards
and see whether the vines have budded,
whether the grape blossoms have opened
and the pomegranates are in bloom.
There I will give you my love.[31]

When we are worshipping the Lord in spirit and truth, our hearts align with His. We have the mind of Christ. We do not need to constantly ask Him what His will is. We know it, because we are one with Him. The bride here takes the initiative. She knows Her lover's longing for the fields that are yet unharvested. She understands His tender heart for the immature vines and fruit trees. Her motivation is that He would be satisfied.

This is the height of worship, when we move as one with our mighty Lord and saviour. We truly become His life partner, His co-worker. It is not that work is the highest form of worship, but simply that love cannot be shown apart from action. Jesus said it this way: ***"If anyone loves me, he will keep my word"***.[32] This is not just hearing His word or even speaking His word, but acting on it, obeying it.

---

31. Song of Songs 7:11-12
32. John 14:23

That is why Paul realised that to worship was to become a *living sacrifice*. As we fall more in love with Jesus, He can share more of His broken heart with us. He is longing for His bride from every tribe and nation. She is in every sector of society. ***She*** may be a drug addict or a president, it does not matter, Jesus is longing for *'her'*.

His love is an unquenchable flame. Ezekiel saw it as he worshipped, and so did John the apostle. The nearest we can describe the glory of our bridegroom in earthly terms is that He is full of fire.[33]

> *Set me as a seal upon your heart,*
> *as a seal upon your arm,*
> *for love is strong as death,*
> *jealousy is fierce as the grave.*
> *Its flashes are flashes of fire,*
> *the very flame of the Lord.*
> *Many waters cannot quench love,*
> *neither can floods drown it.*
> *If a man offered for love*
> *all the wealth of his house,*
> *he would be utterly despised.*[34]

This fire is His passionate love for us. It can never be extinguished. We are like the bush that Moses saw when he first met the Lord. The bush was an ordinary desert shrub,

---

33. Ezekiel 1:26-27; Revelation 1:14-16
34. Song of Songs 8:6-7

nothing special about it. Yet when the Lord came down, it became a means of drawing someone into His presence.

When we worship, we burn with the very fire of God. Yet we are not consumed, simply purified. We are ordinary, unremarkable, and yet we become a means of others seeing the glory of God.

Celebration for the Nations

I have been in Christian work for many years, but I have not always appreciated that our primary calling is to worship. In 2004 I was taking part in a regular prayer day our ministry holds when suddenly I had a vision.

I saw the most beautiful water. The nearest earthly colour to describe it would be a deep sapphire blue. The unusual thing about the water was that light was coming from within it. I tried to touch it, but something blocked my hand. I then looked up and saw that there were many other people, all different nationalities, and all, like me, trying to get to the water.

Then we heard a voice saying, *"It is impossible for you to get to the water, but if you sing it will break out and come to you".* As I heard the voice, a scripture flashed into my mind:

"Gather the people together, so that I may give them water." Then Israel sang this song:

"Spring up, O well!"[35]

I felt the Lord commissioning me to gather people together to worship Him, because He wanted to give us living water. I realised that it was the centenary of the great Welsh Revival. As we prayed over the vision, the Lord started to show us that, wonderful as the 1904 Welsh Revival had been, His intentions for it were never completed, they were blocked up.

What started in Wales, and transformed the society at the time, moved out to many other nations. Welsh missionaries in Northeast India heard what was happening in their homeland and begged the Lord to pour out His Spirit where they were. He came in power in 1905. William Seymour of Azusa Street fame was greatly encouraged by Evan Roberts, the Welsh Revivalist, and the Holy Spirit fell in Los Angeles in 1906. Pyongyang, the capital of what is now North Korea, became the centre of a revival in 1907. Many other places in Europe, the Far East and Australia were touched by revival at the beginning of the twentieth century.

Looking at a map and placing Jerusalem in its centre,[36] the revival that started in Wales went to the ends of the earth. However, before it could flow back from those places into the mainly Islamic, Hindu, Buddhist and Communist nations in the central regions of the world, the First World War started. This war pitted Christian against Christian, and in many cases

---

35. Numbers 21:16-17
36. Ezekiel 5:5

'revived' Christian against 'revived' Christian. Instead of a message of life and love, the enemy swept in with death and destruction.

The First World War caused many in Europe and beyond to question whether there was a God, and, if there was, was He good? At the same time, a religious spirit took hold in many of the churches. Leaders were afraid of some of the excesses of revival, and in a bid to bring order and control often ended up quenching (stifling) the Holy Spirit. This meant that they were in no position to bring answers to their grieving and confused congregations.

The Lord reminded us of the children of Israel. They missed the Lord's purposes the first time around, but He never changed His mind, He still intended them to enter the promised land. Likewise, God had not changed His mind about what He wanted to do in the nations. He had promised through the prophet Joel that He would pour out His Spirit on all people.[37]

We saw that the *wells* of His purpose had got blocked up through our own sin. Yet we also realised that the Lord was giving us a strategy to unblock them. He was calling us to worship, specifically to sing.

I am not a worship leader. I am a missionary and I was trained to depend on prayer and the word of God. Yet the

---

37. Joel 2:28-29

Lord was telling me to gather people from the nations that were touched by the 1904 Welsh Revival so that we could sing together for a week. No teaching, just worship. I was nervous, but I couldn't doubt what the Lord had showed me.

Our Mission HQ is just a few miles from where the 1904 Welsh Revival started. The local council owns a large open area that was built for the 2000 National Eisteddfod (festival) of Wales, so we hired it and planned a village under canvas just outside the town. It took us three years to understand and interpret the vision and then find worshippers from the different nations. **Celebration for the Nations** (a celebration of God's victory on behalf of those who don't yet know it, and can't yet worship Him) took place for a week in the summer of 2007.

It was a relatively small gathering (1,300 worshippers at its peak), and yet we gave ourselves simply to worship the Lord with all our hearts and all our strength. A wonderful leadership team formed. The Korean people came in their hundreds. We were overwhelmed by their zeal and devotion. Some of them had sold computers, guitars, whatever they had, to make the journey. Some who came did not even yet know Jesus personally. They had grown up going to church, and been swept along by the enthusiasm of friends or pastors. We had a team from Northeast India, and Americans, Europeans, Chinese and of course British.

What amazed me was how, day by day, the tent in which

we worshipped was filled with the manifest presence of God. Local people walked in and got saved. A St John Ambulance man whom we had hired to give first aid wept his way to Jesus. Many of the young Korean churchgoers met Jesus personally for the very first time. All we were doing was singing. Yet it was obedience. It was our outpouring of love to our saviour.

Backsliders found faith again. A drunk homeless man made the tent his home for the week and later found salvation, a home and a job. I found out afterwards that although we never gave a call to mission, several trace their missionary journey back to that week. The Lord spoke very personally and individually to people. Often in the tent as many stood in worship, others were on their knees in prayer, or on their faces in repentance.

We are now in our twelfth year of **Celebration for the Nations.** We see it as a worship intercession for revival. One of a myriad of Spirit-led expressions throughout the world at the moment. However, at its heart it is just a minuscule part of the worship that God deserves.

I am sharing this testimony because my involvement with **Celebration for the Nations** has turned my own personal time with the Lord upside down. At least I now believe it has turned it the right way up! Worship first. Worship is more important than the most urgent of requests, because it is our way of putting Jesus first. As I begin to fix my heart on who He is, and allow my soul and my spirit to magnify His name, everything else comes into perspective.

As I worship Him, I see that what I had thought impossible is easy for Him. I am in a place where I can hear His whispers. I really can come into the very Holy of Holies, the throne room of God. I will not be turned away. I can stay as long as I want to, and I have found that the longer I stay, the more productive I am. To worship is to find the most efficient way to work.

Chapter 5
Praying in the Beloved Warrior

Prayer is LOVE listening,
His and mine.
His infinite
And mine in time; impatient.

Prayer is hands touching,
Strength to mine.
And from His weakness
I have found iron, for standing.

Prayer is eyes meeting,
His search mine.
Fiery jewels,
Eternal in time, for building.

Prayer is communion
Face to face,
Wonderful weakness,
Calvary's grace, my dying.

Prayer is LOVE dancing
Arms entwined.
Life in the movement,
Kingdom wine, my living!

Prayer and love cannot be separated. Our God has given us a way to communicate with Him heart to heart because He loves us. It was never meant to be a cold ceremony, or a list of obligations. Prayer is a relationship between us and the Lord of the universe. He does not prescribe a method of prayer, or a set time. In fact, His encouragement to us is to pray continually. That would be impossible unless it were something as natural to the believer as breathing. A living in awareness of Jesus, a living in love.

Paul knew this secret. His letters are full of the little phrase *in Christ.* This is because that is where he learnt to live. That was the secret of his power in prayer and action. He lived in that betrothal relationship I spoke of in Chapter 1. He knew what it was to be one with his beloved. Therefore, his prayer and his action were from that place of oneness, seated with Christ in the heavenly realms.[1]

It meant that when things seemed to go horribly wrong, he would still praise God. He could sit in chains and be in prayer and worship. Centuries later Adoniram Judson, a missionary to Burma, was tortured and imprisoned in the worst possible

---

1. Ephesians 2:6

conditions. A fellow prisoner looking at his chains taunted him by asking what the prospects for the gospel in Burma were now. Judson's reply showed that he too still sat with Christ in the heavenly realms. He said, "The future is as bright as the promises of God".

The word of God is the rock on which we stand in prayer. The word is Christ Himself. Our Beloved Warrior has given us His word, and whatever our circumstances, that word will prevail. Prayer is speaking it, holding it in our hearts, breathing it into the impossible.

This prayer relationship is a two-way flow of life and love. It is our means of bringing the kingdom of heaven into the world in which we live. Yet it is also emotional. We have the ability to bring Jesus delight as we pray, using the authority He gave us through His death. We can know His pain, His longing, His laughter and His victorious joy as we join Him in prayer. Prayer is spirit to Spirit, but also heart to heart.

Holy communion

Prayer is a holy communion. We are invited to sit at the table with Jesus as He breaks the bread and offers it to us. His body broken for us and for the world. We see again His incredible love, as He holds out His gift. He is giving Himself, nothing less. His life for ours.

As we take the bread in our hands, He is silently challenging us to go 'out' in our prayer, and offer this bread to others. We find that it multiplies in our hands. The more we bless others, the more blessing flows freely through us. Yet in giving, in praying, we too are broken. We feel the pain of others. We grieve for the lost. We find in this holy communion that we are the body of Christ. We too must be broken if we are to bring life to the world. In this prayer we begin to realise the mystery of fellowship with Jesus in His suffering.

Yet the communion does not end there. Jesus gives us the cup. The covenant in His blood. This sacrifice is complete. The Lamb of God has poured out His blood so that all sins, all sickness, every work of Satan is defeated. Our part in receiving this cup is not identification, as it was with the bread, but simply faith and thankfulness. This cup is the wine of the kingdom of God. It is our joy. It is the ultimate demonstration of love. Our part is to drink deeply. Prayer is rejoicing in the victory that Jesus has already won.

The blood becomes our weapon. As we look at our lives, we look through the finished work of Christ. We see more than our struggles, our doubts and our fears. We see ourselves cleansed, free, conquerors standing with the One who is more than a conqueror.

As darkness takes hold of our society, and we look at suffering across the world, we stand into a position of hope. We see that the kingdom of God is at hand. The covenant is cut. The cross is enough. The victory is already won. Our prayer is a declaration that Love never fails.

The root of sin

All of this I know, and to some extent experience to be true. And yet sometimes I feel powerless in prayer. I think of my friend who still needs healing, my neighbour struggling with depression. So then when I am praying for bigger things, if I am not careful I can feel undermined.

The Bible tells us that the root of every sin is unbelief. We see that clearly in the teaching Jesus gives to His disciples about the Holy Spirit in those precious days before He goes to the cross.

> *"Nevertheless, I tell you the truth: it is to your advantage that I go away, for if I do not go away, the Helper will not come to you. But if I go, I will send him to you. And when he comes, he will convict the world concerning sin and righteousness and judgement:* ***concerning sin, because they do not believe in me;*** *concerning righteousness, because I go to the Father, and you will see me no longer; concerning judgement, because the ruler of this world is judged."* [2]

One of the ministries of the Holy Spirit is to convict the world of sin. The root of that sin is simple: it is not believing in who Jesus is, and what He has done. Conversely, it is faith that justifies us, and it is by faith that we can please God. Paul teaches us in the book of Romans: *Whatever does not*

---

2. John 16:7-11, emphasis added

proceed from faith is sin.[3]

So then, faith and sin are opposites. To overcome sin we must have faith. Yet how do we rid ourselves of unbelief? So often I feel like the man who asked Jesus to heal his demon possessed son, *"I believe; help my unbelief!"*[4] Faith is there, but so is doubt, and hence so is sin.

This is where the Holy Spirit is such a precious friend. Jesus promised us, *"I will ask the Father, and he will give you another Helper, to be with you for ever"*.[5]

Translators have struggled over the word shown here as **Helper**. The Greek word is ***parakletos***. It carries a wealth of treasure not easily expressed: intercessor, consoler, advocate, someone who comes alongside to help. Jesus said the Holy Spirit would be another parakletos, another besides Himself. Jesus is our advocate and intercessor in heaven, and the Holy Spirit is the same on earth. They are one in character and in love for us. The Holy Spirit is also our Beloved Warrior, come to fight for us and make His home in us.

It is this Holy Spirit who convicts the world of sin which is caused by unbelief. How do I get rid of unbelief? I allow the Spirit of God to fill me and convict me of sin. Conviction is so different from condemnation. The first may make us squirm,

---

3. Romans 14:23
4. Mark 9:24
5. John 14:16

but always gives us a way of escape. The second just makes us feel terrible with no way out. God never condemns us.

It is only as I become aware - by way of the Holy Spirit's conviction - of specific unbelief that I can turn from it. I remember clearly one time when I was travelling in Egypt with a team, we attended a powerful Christian meeting. The speaker challenged us to believe the Lord for any healing we needed. I had suffered with asthma for over ten years. I felt I needed to make a stand and claim my healing by the blood of Jesus. That night I had an asthma attack. I was discouraged, and talked with a friend. He asked simply if I believed that the Lord could heal me. I said that I did. So he challenged me to throw away my inhalers. I soon realised the unbelief that was still in my heart.

I was upset by my own lack of faith, but didn't know how to get rid of my unbelief. I knew that I did not have the faith to throw my medicine away. I realise now that I was experiencing the conviction of the Holy Spirit at that time. I started repenting of my unbelief, and crying out for the Lord to deliver me. I confessed my double-mindedness, knowing that faith and unbelief were coexisting in me.

In a communion service the next day I started, as is my practice, to picture Jesus on the cross. Suddenly the 'picture' came alive. I felt Jesus looking straight at me. He could not speak because He was struggling to breathe. Suddenly I knew with certainty that when He died, He took my asthma into His body and carried it to the grave. I did not have to live with it, because He had died with it! I was free!

After that I joyfully threw my inhalers away. For a few nights the asthma tried to come back, but I came against it with the conviction of faith that I had been given. Jesus had taken it, so it had no hold on me! I have never been troubled by asthma since! Later that year I had to visit one of our teams in a Tibetan area high in the mountains. When I arrived, they gave me a test to see how my lungs were coping with the altitude. They could not believe the readings. My breathing was better than theirs, even though they had been living there and adjusted to that altitude. How precious is the healing touch of Jesus!

How precious too is the conviction of the Holy Spirit. When He shows us our unbelief, He does it for our deliverance.

I would just like to add a word of caution to this testimony. I am not saying that it is wrong to take medicine or receive medical treatment. I am certainly not advocating people throwing their medicines away without a strong conviction to do so. What I am saying is that when we have a word from the Lord about healing, this is an encouragement to press through to the place of faith, and allow the Holy Spirit to root out any unbelief in us.

There is no one alive on earth today who witnessed the crucifixion except the Holy Spirit. He is the eyewitness who comes alongside me and shows me that my sin does not have to hold me, because He saw it dealt with on the cross. He had already witnessed my unbelief about my healing for asthma go into the death of Jesus. When I realised my unbelief, and cried out for His help and deliverance, He revealed it to me. He is your friend too, your advocate, your intercessor. The more we allow Him to free us from unbelief, the more room there is for the faith of the Son of God to dwell in us.

Righteousness

The prayer of a righteous person has great power as it is working. Elijah was a man with a nature like ours, and he prayed fervently that it might not rain, and for three years and six months it did not rain on the earth.[6]

Have you ever, like me, just suffered from a vague sense of unworthiness? It doesn't relate to anything specific, but somehow it interferes with faith in prayer when remembering Scriptures like the one above from James. There is still that little lie that can easily embed itself into our thinking, that Elijah was more righteous than we are.

Here again we can find the Holy Spirit as our precious friend fighting for us. Not only does He convict us of unbelief, but He also convicts us of our righteousness. Let's go back to Jesus teaching about Him:

---

6. James 5:16-17

"And when he comes, he will convict the world concerning sin and righteousness and judgement: concerning sin, because they do not believe in me; **concerning righteousness, because I go to the Father,** *and you will see me no longer."* [7]

Jesus returned to the Father through the painful path to Calvary. It is there that He won our righteousness. Again the Holy Spirit was with Him, witnessing everything. He saw Jesus becoming sin so that everyone who believed in Him could become the righteousness of God.[8]

Of course, when we know that we have sinned, we need to confess our sin and receive the cleansing of the blood of Jesus. Yet often we still carry vague feelings of guilt or a sense of shame. This unspecific guilt and shame is a device of Satan. He is the one who condemns, though he has no legal right to do so. As we allow the Holy Spirit, He will shine a light into our inner being. He will expose the condemnation that Satan tries to lay on us. In that light He will convict, that is convince us of our righteousness. I am righteous because Jesus completed His work on the cross. I walk in righteousness, in the reality of the new creation that Jesus has made me.

So, unless we are living in a deliberate sin, as born-again believers we can be assured that we are righteous. The Holy Spirit will witness to it in our hearts. Therefore our prayer has

---

7. John 16:8-10, emphasis added

8. 2 Corinthians 5:21

great power as it is working.

We need to battle to get the truth inside us. Faith comes by hearing, and hearing the word of God. As we discipline ourselves to read and meditate on God's word, we can ask the Holy Spirit to soak us in the truth of the Scriptures. Then we begin to really see who we are in Christ, and what authority He has shared with us, His bride. Just look at what Jesus says:

"Have faith in God. Truly, I say to you, whoever says to this mountain, 'Be taken up and thrown into the sea,' and does not doubt in his heart, but believes that what he says will come to pass, it will be done for him. Therefore I tell you, whatever you ask in prayer, believe that you have received it, and it will be yours".[9]

How powerful this prayer of faith is! Jesus did not tell us to ask Him to move the mountain, but told us that we ourselves, by faith in Him, could move mountains.

So often in prayer we ask Him to do what He died to give us the right to do. We suffer because we don't understand who we are. As we allow the Holy Spirit to have His way, we can stop death and destruction from ravaging our streets. He shows us that prayer is so much more than a series of requests. He leads us to enter into the dynamic relationship which releases the power of heaven onto the earth.

---

9. Mark 11:22-24

Judgement

The Holy Spirit can convict or convince us of who we truly are. He will also convict us of one more thing:

*"And when he comes, he will convict the world concerning sin and righteousness and judgement ... concerning judgement, **because the ruler of this world is judged**".*[10]

He convicts us of our sin and righteousness, and of Satan's judgement. The NIV puts it this way: *"**the prince of this world now** stands condemned"* (emphasis added). At the cross we were set free, but Satan was judged and condemned. His authority was taken from him. He was the prince of this world, but when Jesus rose again, He declared, *"**All authority in heaven and on earth has been given to me**".*[11]

Satan no longer has authority on earth or in heaven. His weapons were taken from him when Jesus died:

*God made [us] alive together with him, having forgiven us all our trespasses, by cancelling the record of debt that stood against us with its legal demands. This he set aside, nailing it to the cross. **He disarmed the rulers and authorities and put them to open***

---

10. John 16:8 & 11, emphasis added

11. Matthew 28:18, emphasis added

shame, by triumphing over them in him.[12]

Yet Satan still holds billions captive. He still causes untold suffering. How? His power is in the tongue. His power is the counterfeit of the living word of God, it is the power of lies. With lies he controls the minds of people, stirring up jealousy and hatred. With lies he destroys marriages, lures the vulnerable, panders to the power-crazed and creates false religions.

His lies lead to a state of lawlessness. Men and women turn aside from the law that is written on their conscience and that is manifest in the created world. They reject God's commandments and become victims of what is perverse. Jesus spoke of this lawlessness growing strongly in the last days and warned: ***"And because lawlessness will be increased, the love of many will grow cold".***[13]

When we love God, we obey His commandments and prosper. When we disobey His commandments, love grows cold and hatred will reign.

Our weapon is the truth, the word of God. His way, His law, His kingdom. Jesus knew that the battle would be fierce. He did not leave us as helpless orphans. His Holy Spirit is a warrior like Him. He convicts us that the enemy is defeated, so that no matter what the situation looks like, we can proclaim

---

12. Colossians 2:13-15, emphasis added

13. Matthew 24:12

the truth. Love wins!

If we will allow the Holy Spirit, our helper, to do what He was sent to do for us, our love will not grow cold. We will become more and more convicted of who we really are. Day by day He will teach us how to use God's word in prayer and speak to the mountains. We really don't know how to pray as we ought, but the Holy Spirit intercedes for us.[14] He is our interpreter! Through Him we begin to understand the kingdom of heaven that has been planted within us. Through Him we can share that kingdom with others.

Prayer for a king

First of all, then, I urge that supplications, prayers, intercessions, and thanksgivings be made for all people, for kings and all who are in high positions, that we may lead a peaceful and quiet life, godly and dignified in every way.[15]

This Scripture came to our minds as just two of us were struggling to have a day of prayer in a Muslim nation. We had been used to 30 or 40 people praying together, worshipping, sharing the word. Now we were thousands of miles away from our friends.

We tentatively started to bless the King of the land.

---

14. Romans 8:26

15. 1 Timothy 2:1-2

Suddenly a prayer of obedience came alive, and Scriptures started to flow from our hearts. We got excited, recognising the gentle tug of the Holy Spirit as He led us towards the heart of the Father for this King. He was a man with weaknesses and struggles, yet carrying a great responsibility. He was not a good man in our judgement, yet we were filled with a conviction of the Lord's love for him.

Two young women in a small village praying for a king. What difference could we make? Yet, we dared to believe that as daughters of the King of kings we had authority. The prayer stayed in our hearts. We didn't pray it every day, but at times it became a deep longing. We asked others to join this prayer. We prayed for the King's salvation, yet we felt no witness about this.

We remembered what Paul said to Timothy: to pray for these leaders so that the people they ruled could know peace and godliness. We began to ask the Lord to use this King to open the nation to the gospel in some way. As crazy as it sounded to pray that a Muslim king would allow the gospel entrance to his nation, we found that this prayer registered deep within us.

Year by year we held this prayer in our hearts. Though we saw no evidence of any kind of breakthrough with it, we felt that we were praying what Jesus Himself was asking the Father.

Then suddenly, on a visit to another nation, the King made

a stunning announcement on the radio. He recommended to his ex-patriot people in that land that they read the gospel of Matthew. A little while later we heard that the King had decreed that Bibles could be sold in the bookshops in his land! We saw evidence of this in the city near us: a general bookshop displaying a Bible for sale in the window!

Our teams and many others no longer needed to smuggle Bibles in. For several months the country was open to the Scriptures. When the window of opportunity shut, due to pressure from other Muslim leaders, we were sad, and yet thrilled to know that many thousands, and probably tens of thousands, of Bibles and gospels had been distributed.

The king's heart is a stream of water in the hand of the Lord; he turns it wherever he will.[16]

We had prayed, and the Lord had moved His hand!

---

16. Proverbs 21:1

Chapter 6
Being the voice of the Beloved Warrior

Find your voice.
You speak so many words, but find your voice.
Only in the silence can you hear.
Listen to the stillness.
Wait.

The noise must die.
The gentle calling comes, the quiet trust.
The earthquake, wind and fire just destroy,
I call you to bring life,
Wait.

Your heart with Mine.
The throb of Heaven is a word on earth.
Your heart will overflow as Mine does still
Your voice declares My will,
Create.

When the Israelites were in the wilderness, the Lord provided everything they needed. Though the life they had was not easy, it was secure. There was always manna to eat, all they had to do was gather it. Yet generally, in the wilderness they were not 'speaking' for the Lord. Their 'voice' was not heard; they had no testimony until they were led into battle.

It is the same for us Christians. We can gather our manna daily and go about our lives. We can be nice, have lovely fellowship together, arrange lots of meetings and events, yet have very little impact on the society around us. Why? We are not taking land for the gospel. We are not going into battle.

Paul reminds us in Ephesians 6 that our battle is not with people, but with powers and principalities. How do we overcome our enemy?

*And they have conquered him by the **blood** of the Lamb and by the **word** of their testimony, for they **loved not their lives** even unto death.*[1]

We exalt the Lamb, and His victory on the cross! We remind each other that the cross is enough! The blood of Jesus has cleansed us and given us eternal, overcoming life. This is the battle cry of worship. Jesus has done the work, He has won the war; our job is to proclaim it!

---

1. Revelation 12:11, emphasis added

This is our testimony as we take the land. It is not possible to take new ground without a weapon. Jesus has put a sword in our hand. It is the word He has spoken into our hearts, the word of our testimony, the word for which we are ready to die.

*Take the helmet of salvation, and **the sword of the Spirit, which is the word of God**, praying at all times in the Spirit, with all prayer and supplication.*[2]

Our weapon is made of the same substance that created the universe. With it we bring the kingdom that has always existed, the kingdom of God, into this world of time and space. It is Spirit Word. It is Jesus Himself. His being, His promises, His purpose.

In the beginning was the Word.[3]

As I mentioned before, the Greek for *word is logos.* It is a very powerful concept embodying the spoken word but also the reason, or meaning, behind it. It could well be translated: *In the beginning was the meaning.*

God spoke meaning into chaos when He created the world. He is still speaking meaning into chaos in our fallen world. He calls us to speak with Him.

---

2. Ephesians 6:17-18, emphasis added

3. John 1:1

The word of our testimony

Testimony in the New Testament is the same as the word for 'witness' or 'martyr'. Our testimony is our witness of what the Lord has said to, or done for, us. In its truest sense it really is the word for which we are prepared to die. So often we think of testimony as an account of our salvation. It is that, but so much more. It is more even than our sharing of daily blessings and deliverances. It is also that word that our Lord has spoken to us, and that we stand on and speak out, even though we may not yet have seen the outworking. Our testimony is that God is faithful, and that His word will produce the fruit.

Joshua had a promise from the Lord. He was told that wherever he put his foot, that land would be his. The root of his name is the same as the root of the name of Jesus. It means salvation. Joshua was a forerunner of Jesus. Jesus put His foot on the head of Satan when He died on the cross[4]. In defeating Satan, Jesus received back the land that Satan had stolen... the nations of the world.

We come into the good of what Jesus did on the cross, and like Joshua, are given the same promise. If we will put our feet on the ground and take a place for the kingdom of God, it will be given to us.

So, let's see how Joshua did it.

---

4. Genesis 3:15

Being God's voice

Testimony goes before us and prepares the way. Moses and Joshua had lived a life of obedience to God's word. The results were that the people of Canaan were already in fear of them, even before they had invaded! Listen to what Rahab tells the spies Joshua sent to Jericho:

"I know that the Lord has given you the land, and that the fear of you has fallen upon us, and that all the inhabitants of the land melt away before you. For we have heard how the Lord dried up the water of the Red Sea before you when you came out of Egypt, and what you did to the two kings of the Amorites who were beyond the Jordan, to Sihon and Og, whom you devoted to destruction".[5]

We need to know that when we are walking in obedience to the Lord, the demons are already terrified of us. Our obedience becomes a testimony on the lips of our enemies.

Joshua had been told to lead the people into the land of Canaan. God had promised that as He had been with Moses, so He would be with Joshua. Joshua's first big test of faith was the Jordan river. He had a testimony from 40 years before, when he had seen the Red Sea part as Moses obeyed the Lord, and held up his hand. Now there was a river in full flood that was an obstacle to them entering the land.

---

5. Joshua 2:9-10

Joshua was Moses' disciple. Moses had taught him to listen to the Lord, not simply to copy what he did. Joshua did not stand in front of the Jordan with his right hand stretched out, commanding the water back as Moses had done. It was a new day, and there was a different strategy.

Joshua had always stayed by the tent of meeting. He knew what it was to seek the presence of the Lord. God is His word. He cannot be separated from Himself. Joshua's success came because He obeyed the Lord, and meditated on His word day and night.[6] So the Lord spoke a fresh word to him:

"And as for you, command the priests who bear the ark of the covenant, 'When you come to the brink of the waters of the Jordan, you shall stand still in the Jordan'".[7]

This new day was one on which they would be physically taking ground. God's word to them was all about where they put their feet to take that ground. The priests had to *stand* in the middle of a river which was in flood! Their confidence was that they were carrying the ark, the presence of God. Still, they had no idea what would happen.

It was only as they began to walk into the Jordan that they too became the 'voice' of the Lord. They saw the miracle happen as they placed their feet on the ground they wanted

---

6. Joshua 1:8

7. Joshua 3:8

to take. They were proclaiming that God's word is true!

> *"Every place that the sole of your foot will tread upon I have given to you."* [8]

Our promised land

Some old hymns would have us believe that our promised land only comes to us when we die and go to heaven. Yet we are children of Abraham.

> *For the promise to Abraham and his offspring that he would be **heir of the world** did not come through the law but through the righteousness of faith.* [9]

We are heirs of this world too! Jesus has got all authority in heaven and on earth. Joshua won the land by physical battle. Our call, since the cross, is to spiritual battle, the battle for souls. Yet the weapon for both is the same: the sword of the Spirit, the word of God.

Joshua spoke his instructions to the people, and so became the voice of the Lord to the nation. Most of us are not in a position to speak to a nation, but we can speak into our neighbourhood or our place of work. We can speak to that person that we just can't get out of our mind. Are there not things that the Holy Spirit is putting in our hearts? As we

---

8. Joshua 1:3

9. Romans 4:13, emphasis added

believe Him, we can speak out, in prayer first, and then, as He leads us, in action, and become God's voice. Isn't that how any new ground is taken for the Lord?

Jericho

I wonder how Joshua felt as he looked up at the walls of Jericho? Have you ever followed a vision to the point when the 'reality' of what you were doing faced you, and suddenly all your dreams were challenged? *Did God really say...? Maybe I misunderstood...? Maybe it is not for now?*

It seems to me that everything that makes a difference for the kingdom of God goes through this stage. John Wimber famously said that faith is spelt R-I-S-K. Satan will always try to silence the word of God. He knows that when it is spoken in faith, miracles happen. Very often our 'speaking' is an action. As James said,

But someone will say, "You have faith and I have works." Show me your faith apart from your works, and I will show you my faith by my works.[10]

God had said to Joshua that He would give him the land where he put his feet. It was time to get feet on the ground in Jericho. Yet how could that be when Jericho was surrounded by walls that seemed as though they reached the sky?

---

10. James 2:18

I am so grateful that the Lord does not leave us once He has given us His word. He is not our boss giving us a job to do and expecting us just to get on with it. He is our Father, training us, disciplining us, encouraging us to come into the authority that is our inheritance.

So He didn't just leave Joshua looking at the walls of Jericho in a battle for faith, He met him there. *When Joshua was by Jericho, he lifted up his eyes and looked, and behold, a man was standing before him with his drawn sword in his hand. And Joshua went to him and said to him, "Are you for us, or for our adversaries?" And he said, "No; but I am the commander of the army of the Lord. Now I have come." And Joshua fell on his face to the earth and worshipped and said to him, "What does my lord say to his servant?" And the commander of the Lord's army said to Joshua, "Take off your sandals from your feet, for the place where you are standing is holy." And Joshua did so.*[11]

The Commander of the army of the Lord! We now know His name: it is Jesus! The focus of Joshua's attention shifted from the impossible walls, to the One who is the Lord of hosts. Joshua knew he was seeing the Lord and he worshipped Him.

We don't know all that went on between them on that holy ground, but when Joshua emerged, he knew what to do. He had met with the living Word of God. The word that God had spoken to him before he entered Canaan had been re-

---

11. Joshua 5:13-15

breathed by the Saviour.

We too can seek and expect these holy times of intimacy with God as we do our best to walk in obedience to His word. He does not give His word without His presence, it is the sword of the *Spirit*, the word of God. Unless we have these times when we take off our shoes (that is, to set aside the attempts to fulfil His commands in our own strength), we will never fully enter in to all that He can do through us.

Joshua was now in a position to put his feet on the ground that he knew the Lord would give him. Jesus had 'kissed' him with the word. He had breathed it into him. Now he had the strength to lead the nation into something that seemed stupid in the eyes of the world. He told them to make themselves totally vulnerable to all the weapons the inhabitants of Jericho could muster, by walking around the walls. Surely the people of Jericho had prepared heavy stones, bows and arrows and many other methods of resisting attack?

God's people Israel were speaking out their testimony, they became the voice of the Lord. They were declaring by their action that the Lord would give them the city, they were living out the word and marching around it. For six days they marched around the city in silence. Each day I am sure faith was building in the people. No one had attacked them, not one stone had been thrown. Perhaps the Lord knew that if He had allowed them to speak before they began to experience the miracle, their voices would have been full of doubt. It is always wiser to stay silent than speak in doubt or fear.

On the seventh day, the Sabbath, on which under normal circumstances they were commanded to rest, the Lord had them march around Jericho seven times! It was the nation's equivalent of what had happened to Joshua. They too were now on holy ground. Figuratively speaking they were taking their shoes off. They were entering into the Sabbath of God when they rested from their own works, their own ideas and strengths, and entirely depended upon Him and His word.

The seventh time they circled Jericho, Joshua commanded the trumpets to sound and then said to the people, ***"Shout, for the Lord has given you the city"***.[12]

What a glorious moment when a nation was so in line with the thoughts of God that its people's voice became His voice! Their testimony, His testimony. For the testimony of Jesus is the spirit of prophecy![13] The Lord had surely given them the city! The walls that had seemed to reach the sky crumbled to the ground. The people marched in.

Our voice, His voice

We are created to speak the words of God on earth, and by doing that to see His kingdom coming through our faith and obedience. We are the body of Christ; thus we are also

---

12. Joshua 6:16, emphasis added
13. Revelation 19:10

His voice to those who have never yet heard Him.

In Revelation, when John saw and heard the Lord, he described His voice like *the sound of rushing waters*.[14] God's voice is a river of life wherever it is heard.

Amazingly, when we see the bride in Revelation 19:6, after she has overcome the enemy, John describes her in this way:

*Then I heard what sounded like a great multitude, like **the roar of rushing waters** and like loud peals of thunder, shouting: "Hallelujah! For our Lord God Almighty reigns".*[15]

When we as the bride walk in our heavenly anointing, our voice is as His voice. We speak His words that are spirit and life. Living waters overflow from our hearts through our mouths. We too make the desert bloom with our faith, our prayer and our praise.

The sound of rushing waters[16] and the roar of rushing waters[17] is the same Greek word, pronounced *'fona'*. It appears again on the day of Pentecost when the disciples started to speak in other tongues. The people were drawn

---

14. Revelation 1:15, NIV

15. Revelation 19:6, NIV, emphasis added

16. Revelation 1

17. Revelation 19

to the *fona*, which means sound but also light. The disciples' voice had become the voice of the Lord which is sound and light, and thousands found salvation!

Jesus taught us that out of the overflow of the heart, the mouth speaks.[18] He had said to his disciples that when the Holy Spirit came, He would overflow from their hearts like rivers of living water.[19] Those rivers had to find an outlet, and they did for the first time on the day of Pentecost. They have done so ever since through every faithful child of God.

I believed, therefore I have spoken

We speak out of what we believe, whether to life or to death. We can speak ourselves into defeat as the Israelites found out the first time they tried to enter Canaan. Or we can speak faith.

Have you noticed the power of speaking out the truth? Somehow keeping truth inside does not have the same effect. There is something about the breath. We are created from word and breath and clay. God said, **"Let us make man in our image"**.[20] He then formed us out of clay and breathed into us[21], so that we could really bear His image. Nothing else in all creation received His breath, it was simply spoken into being.

---

18. Matthew 12:34
19. John 7:38-39
20. Genesis 1:26
21. Genesis 2:7

So, we are made from earth, word and breath (spirit) and we are given authority over the earth as we live from word and spirit. The word is not enough, it must be infused with the life of the One who spoke it. When we receive a word, it is not enough just to keep it inside. At the right time we must speak it out. Word must become an action.

The apostle Paul understood this. In 2 Corinthians 4 he speaks of *the gospel of the glory of Christ*. This was his testimony. In other letters he spoke about it as *my* gospel. The word of God had consumed him and become a part of him and he could not help but speak it out.[22]

He realised what a great treasure we have been given in this gospel, even though our bodies are like jars of clay. In the light of this, the sufferings we face - though they may seem harsh - are in reality light and momentary. He saw that all our struggles are for a greater purpose: So death is at work in us, but life in you.[23]

There is great opposition to the word of God, but nothing can chain it, not even death! So Paul would not be silenced:

Since we have the same spirit of faith according to what has been written, 'I believed, and so I spoke', we also believe, and so we also speak.[24]

---

22. 1 Corinthians 9:16
23. 2 Corinthians 4:12
24. 2 Corinthians 4:13

We too must choose: will we be silenced? The only way to overcome is to not love our lives, even to the point of death. Much of the world is still waiting to hear a message that is backed with that reality.

The Spirit and the bride say, 'Come'

The book of Revelation speaks in its final chapter of complete harmony between the Spirit and the bride. The Holy Spirit is working to help us now to come into this place of agreement. This word 'Come' is a command! The bride, with the Spirit, is calling to Jesus to do their bidding. Incredibly Jesus replies... Yes! He says, ***"Surely I am coming soon".***[25]

We are being trained for greatness. Jesus is not looking for a docile helpmate, but someone who will rule and reign with Him for eternity. Right from the beginning He created us to have dominion. He asked Adam to name the animals, because Adam had authority over them. Adam spoke, and so it was.

Our ability to reign has been corrupted by the Fall. The world's way to have authority is so different to God's way. Yet as we co-operate with the Holy Spirit, He will teach us how to reign now, on earth. Our reigning in life is to do with the authority of our word. We can speak out (shout and sing out) what we know to be true, even when the situation we are faced with causes our words to sound ridiculous. We agree with the Spirit, and that word becomes our testimony.

---

25. Revelation 22:20

We listen to what is going on in heaven, and speak that on to earth. This is wonderful. And yet I think that there is even more. As we abide in the Lord and are one with Him, He gives us authority to do things our own way. We become those who form and create alongside Him. He trusts what He has breathed into us. He allows us to add our personality to it. He encourages us to act out of who we are, uniquely in Him. Smith Wigglesworth punched cancer out of patients, and it left them! Others lay hands on in a gentler way.

Joshua saw that he needed more time to defeat the enemy in one particular battle. He was walking in the authority that the Lord had given him to take the land. So, with no record of a specific word from God, he commanded the sun, and it stood still. He stopped the universe at his word! As he walked in obedience to the purposes of God for his life, his word became the word of the Lord.

Peter told the Lord Jesus to invite him to come to Him on the water if indeed He wasn't a ghost. Jesus invited him to come, and Peter initiated a miracle and walked (if only for a brief time) on water.

We cannot have authority until we are under authority. Yet, if we will learn to abide in Christ, I believe that He invites us to initiate things, and gives us a lot of choice about how to do it.

*"If you abide in me, and my words abide in you, **ask***

***whatever you wish**, and it will be done for you."* [26]

The key is love. The Lord will not give His seal to any word of ours that is not rooted in love. He is the Beloved Warrior, and if we will walk with Him we will discover that we too are beloved warriors. That our word and His word are aligned. That we agree with Him, but incredibly, that He too will agree with us!

Learning to reign

I was so excited when I first came into Christian work. I knew I was going to live by faith, so as a student I tried (without much success) to save money from my student grant! It took someone else to point out the incongruity of saving up, to live by faith!

I also treated myself in my last few weeks at university to a cream cake every week, as I reasoned that when I lived by faith I wouldn't be able to afford any. Actually within weeks of me starting at (what later became) a worldwide mission movement called World Horizons, we had come to an arrangement with a nice lady at the local bakers to get all their unsold produce at the end of the day. Cream cakes were in abundance!

I don't think my heavenly Father was mad at me for my lack of faith; in fact I am sure He had a good chuckle. However, I say this to illustrate how flawed my image of God

---

26. John 15:7, emphasis added

was, and yet He still looked after me. His voice still holds sway, even when ours falters.

Once in those early months, we completely ran out of money, and had nothing with which to buy food. There were five of us and we were all praying, commanding, speaking out the promises of provision in God's word. This was our testimony, this was our weapon. Yet our attention was fixed on the morning post. We were sure that some money would arrive in a letter. When letters arrived our spirits rose, and yet none of them had any money.

The day passed in discouragement. No money, no food; this life of faith wasn't working. My father had told me that I would be back in a couple of months asking for his help, and it looked as though he was right.

That night there was a knock on the door. When we opened it we saw a couple whom we didn't know holding a very large box. They smiled and told us that they had just moved into the area to pastor one of the local churches. They had heard about a Christian team which was working in the town, and wanted to bless us. We invited them in and they set the box on the table. It was full of food. Not only necessities, but luxuries. We laughed and cried as we saw the goodness of the Lord. His way.

The Lord was teaching me to trust Him for my own needs. The ground I was taking for Him was in my own soul. This is always where our journey begins. You may not 'live by faith' in trusting the Lord for your daily food, but in fact the Lord offers every believer a life of faith. It is not just saving faith that we need, but daily living faith. We learn first of all to take ground in our own lives. To speak out our testimony that we are forgiven, so that we will not be tripped up by condemnation. To speak forgiveness, so that we will not be mired in bitterness. To declare who we are: beloved sons and daughters of the Father, so that we will not care too much what others say about us. To revel in the love of our bridegroom, so that we cast out all fear.

As we learn to maintain that ground, we can also speak truth over and, when we get the opportunity, *to* those around us. Intentional, loving prayer and witness from every member of the body of Christ would revolutionise this world!

A mentor of mine once illustrated the life of faith to me as we were having breakfast together. He set different things from the table in a line, the smallest first, ending with the cereal box. He told me that the Lord takes us stage by stage. He will always put challenges in front of us, things that to us seem impossible. We jump with Him over the first obstacle and learn to trust Him more. The obstacles get bigger and bigger, not because God is mean, but because He wants us to learn how much bigger He is. He wants to increase our area of authority, so that we can take the inheritance He has prepared for us. When we jump the cereal box there will still be bigger challenges, until we are finally caught up with Jesus in the air.

So, let me tell you about my 'cereal box'. I mentioned in Chapter 4 the vision God gave me for what we called **Celebration for the Nations**. As I spoke the vision out, others who had heard similar things from God gathered. We didn't know how to go about gathering worshippers from all over the world to our little town of Llanelli in South Wales, so we simply started to pray and proclaim and worship together. We believed, therefore we spoke!

We had no idea how many people to prepare for, or how much it would cost. What we did know is that the Lord had told us to have an open door for all who wanted to come, whatever faith - or no faith - they had. That meant to us that we could not set a ticket price as we would normally do at a conference.

We felt that we should be in a marquee, where anyone could come and go as they wanted to. The Lord showed us that what we were doing was like the Feast of Tabernacles, where the people of Israel were commanded to build booths and rejoice for a week.[27] We were celebrating in advance the final ingathering of the harvest of the nations. Celebrating the victory that Jesus had already won.

Ezekiel was told to prophesy to the winds to come and

---

27. Deuteronomy 16:13-14

breathe on the dead bones that they may live.[28] Our ministry was beginning to have strong links with Korea. I felt I must go to Korea and 'prophesy to the east wind' to come and blow on the 'dead bones' of Wales and Europe. Through a very humble and anointed worship leader who later became my co-leader in this work, God gave me great favour. I was able to speak out in meetings. I found myself being God's voice, my British reserve in abeyance.

When I had tried to estimate how much the Celebration would cost, I had come up with a figure of around £8,000. Finance is not my strong point! Actually what we eventually needed was around £90,000! We were virtually building a village for a week on a couple of fields. We decided we would go for a marquee to hold up to 1,500 people. We would charge for a place to sleep in one of our camping tents, but we determined to keep it to £5 per night.

I struggled, not only with how we would pay the bills, but also about whether it was right to spend so much money on a gathering to worship. I thought about what that money could do in some of the poorer parts of the world where friends and colleagues of mine were working.

On top of that, people were telling us that we had to have speakers, or no one would come. They said that people would lose their voices after the first few days singing, which is why worship conferences are only usually 3-4 days.

---

28. Ezekiel 37:9

Thank God that He brought strong leaders and a team around me, or I know I would have been defeated by all the obstacles. We kept worshipping and praying, and the Lord continued to encourage us.

We had to book the marquee, costing thousands of pounds. Then there was lighting, a PA system, security, legal requirements, health and safety, equipment hire, food, accommodation, the list went on. Yet the team grew and people volunteered to take different responsibilities.

We started to meet in the early morning on the field where the Celebration would be held. We declared God's will. We called to worshippers from the four corners of the earth. We called **Celebration for the Nations** into being. The Lord told us, 'Create with me'. We realised that we too could speak things into existence. We were His children, and He was training us.

One morning, we were on the field very early as the sun was coming up. The field was full of dew, countless droplets sparkling in the rising sun. God's promise filled our hearts:

Your troops will be willing
on your day of battle.
Arrayed in holy splendour,
your young men will come to you
like dew from the morning's womb.[29]

---

29. Psalm 110:3, NIV

We had been praying particularly for young people to find the Lord and find their purpose in life; here was the Lord's answer... They would come!

And come they did! Saved and unsaved. Hundreds of young people, some of whom met the Lord for the first time.

But what about that £90,000 we needed? As we prayed and drew others into our vision, people started to give in quite amazing ways. We were also able to get a couple of grants. We booked the marquee and equipment with down payments, believing (most of the time) that all the money would come in. I say most of the time, because I realised that I had started to clench my jaw at night. I would wake up in the morning with my face aching from the tension. The responsibility was getting to me. I kept putting it back on the Lord, telling Him it was His work, but minutes later tension would build in me again.

Yet, in the midst of the battle there was such a sense of joy. I knew that the Lord had spoken to me, and so, if it came to it, I would sell my house. I still had a mortgage, and the sale would not be able to cover all our debts, but it was the best I could do.

The week of the Celebration came, and we still had outstanding debts of around £40,000. Not only that, but the floors we had put down in the tents for sleeping began to sink, because the ground was so wet from the previous week's rain!

Churches came to the rescue, offering their floors for many to sleep on. Others still braved the elements, and we laid more flooring over the floor that had sunk. For Koreans who are used to hot summers and underfloor heating in the winter, it was truly a sacrifice. Some still talk of that time as the coldest they have ever been. However, the atmosphere was full of joy.

We had decided to take offerings, yet before we even started, people who had travelled from the other side of the world came to give us gifts. One couple had just got married. They offered their wedding money! They have since become part of the leadership team. Business people made pledges. Everybody wanted to give!

As we worshipped, more and more money came in. By the fifth day all our expenses were covered! We had to ask people to stop giving! However, the Lord was touching hearts. He was healing, saving, calling people, and they just wanted to give. We ended the week with over £10,000 surplus that we could give to other ministries.

Was it worth £90,000 to put on this week of worship? The Lord spoke to us from the story of the woman who anointed Him at Bethany:

And when the disciples saw it, they were indignant, saying, "Why this waste? For this could have been sold for a large sum and given to the poor." But Jesus, aware of this, said to them, "Why do you trouble the woman? ***For she has done a***

beautiful thing to me".[30]

Jesus received our worship and He was blessed. As we raised our voices to worship Him, He poured out a spirit of prayer and we became His voice to a waiting world. Whether we would continue to be that was up to each person, but twelve years later, as we continue to worship, I can testify that many have.

---

30. Matthew 26:8-10, emphasis added

Chapter 7
Standing in the Beloved Warrior

Something rests deep down inside me,
Through the turmoil it stays firm,
Panic, doubt, fear grip my feelings
And I question all I've known...

Revelation, wisdom, guidance,
Do I know, or am I wrong?
Chaos puts its hand upon me
And my heart has lost its song.

Is it only by emotion
I've been guided, tossed and thrown?
Or has there been something deeper,
Something that my Lord will own?

Something rests deep down inside me,
Through the turmoil it stays firm,
It's the word my Saviour planted
And His word has found a home.

I have found the greatest treasure
Storms may crash, my heart may groan,
But His Life, His Word is in me
I am His and He's my own.

He has called, yes, He has spoken,
And though my Red Sea seems vast,
I'll believe His hand will guide me
Through the doubts and fears, at last...

To the land which He has promised
To the people He has known
To the field that's ripe for harvest
To the glory, all His own.

Then one day I'll take my treasure
Back into its heavenly home
Lay it at His feet rejoicing
And I'll know as I am known.

Having done all, stand! This is Paul's instruction for when we are wrestling with spiritual powers of darkness. I wrote this poem out of the turmoil of emotions I was battling just before I set off to live in North Africa. I knew God's calling, but it didn't stop the doubts and fears from assailing me. I very nearly gave up - in fact I did for a couple of miserable months. But having done all, I stood on that word that was deep inside me. The armour of God enables us to do that one thing, to stand.

*Therefore take up the whole armour of God, that you may be able to **withstand** in the evil day, and having done all, to **stand** firm.*[1]

I used to think that standing was something passive, that we stood still while God did all the work. However, I have come to realise that standing is very active. The Lord asks us to take a stand. Taking a stand often means action. Action with a purpose. I see now that my stand on my call to North Africa meant action, it meant I had to go there. When we make a stand for anything, we do it because we believe it is right. Our Father asks us to stand for Him, to stand for His kingdom, to stand for His Son.

We are warriors putting a stake in the ground saying, *I will take this for the kingdom, and the enemy is not going to have it back!* The ground could be an unreached tribe, a local school, or a moral cause. The key is that the Lord has spoken to us about it, and so we make our stand. So, let's look at the armour that enables us to stand.

Truth

Stand therefore, having fastened on the belt of truth.[2]

Truth as a belt. How easy it is to get carried away in our zeal for the Lord. I cringe when I think of some of the things I have thought, and sometimes even declared, the Lord has

---

1. Ephesians 6:13, emphasis added
2. Ephesians 6:14

told me to do. For a while I was carried along with excitement, but there was no substance in the word. It was my word, my thoughts, my wishful thinking, and sometimes my pride.

We open ourselves to deep disappointment and confusion if we are not willing to test the word of God in our own hearts, and with others to whom we choose to submit. I praise God for the loving counsellors around me who have not judged me or tried to curb my enthusiasm, but have smiled with me at my mistakes. In my turn I try to be that person for others. Sometimes we need help putting our belt on!

Yet when God speaks, there is that something, that witness inside who will not be silent. Yes, there is opposition, but the One who is the truth has planted a seed of truth inside us, and we know that it will change our lives and the lives of others.

Jesus used the analogy of a seed when He spoke about His word, and how we receive it, in the parable of the sower. He used it with good reason. The seed is not the fruit. A word from Him must be treasured so that it will grow, as Mary, Jesus' mother, knew. As it grows we begin to see its shape, and then we can take our stand. It is easy to misinterpret the truth if we are trying to understand it from the seed. God is never in such a hurry as we are.

This belt of truth is a beautiful thing. It is the whole counsel of God, recorded for us in the Scriptures. It is the word of the One who is the Word, the logos, the meaning. And it is the breathed word of the Holy Spirit, the rhema as He plants these seeds in our hearts. This belt cannot be one and not the other. Jesus Himself told us that the rhema was our daily bread:

"Man shall not live by bread alone, but by every word (rhema) that comes from the mouth of God".[3]

Righteousness

(H)aving put on the breastplate of righteousness.[4]

This precious piece is given as a breastplate over our hearts. If we have any doubt about our righteousness it is really difficult to stand, because we open ourselves up to the enemy's darts of accusation and lies.

Of course, we know that it is not our righteousness, but Jesus'. Thank God that He does not depend on how good we are! However, we need to remember to 'put on' this breastplate.

To take a stand, we must live continually turning our face towards the Lord. The biblical concept of repentance is simply that: to turn away from things, from people, from situations, and turn to the Lord. Repentance does not happen with

---

3. Matthew 4:4

4. Ephesians 6:14

words alone, but with a turning. The Lord is always there, always present with us, but we often need to turn a little to see Him.

Moses was living as a shepherd, keeping his father-in-law's sheep. He had messed up. He had tried to help a fellow Israelite who was being beaten by an Egyptian, and ended up killing the Egyptian. He had to run from his position as a prince in Egypt, and go and live in the wilderness. Then one day he saw a strange sight: a fire in a bush that did not consume the bush.

> *And Moses said, "**I will turn** aside to see this great sight, why the bush is not burned". **When the Lord saw that he turned** aside to see, God called to him out of the bush, "Moses, Moses!" And he said, "Here I am."* [5]

That 'fire' is never far from each one of us. It is the holy presence of God who loves to draw near to His people. Just as Moses had to turn from his daily routine so, if we will do so, we too will hear the Lord calling our name.

This turning is really a 're-turning' to the One who created us. It is a remembering of who we really are. Surely Moses at that time was in something of an identity crisis. He had been brought up as an Egyptian, yet knew he was Hebrew. He felt a desire to help his native people, but when he had tried to, it

---

5. Exodus 3:3-4, emphasis added

had gone horribly wrong. He had been a prince, and now he was a humble shepherd. Who was he really?

When Moses turned to the Lord he began to understand something of his own identity.

"I am the God of your father, the God of Abraham, the God of Isaac, and the God of Jacob." [6]

The Lord was rooting Moses into family, into promise and into covenant. The Lord had made a covenant with Abraham and his offspring:

Then the Lord said to Abram, "Know for certain that your offspring will be sojourners in a land that is not theirs and will be servants there, and they will be afflicted for four hundred years. But I will bring judgement on the nation that they serve, and afterward they shall come out with great possessions." [7]

Once Moses began to grasp that this was the Lord of the covenant, and he was a son of the covenant, he could start to come to terms with what the Lord was asking him to do.

When we turn to the Lord, He does the same for us. He roots us into His family, into His promises, and into His eternal

---

6. Exodus 3:6
7. Genesis 15:13-14

covenant. He shows us that we are called, not because of our righteousness, but because of the love of the righteous one. We need to 're-turn' again and again to where we belong.

In that place of belonging is righteousness, our breastplate. Just as ultimately Jesus is our belt of truth, so also He is our breastplate of righteousness.

The gospel of peace

(A)nd, as shoes for your feet, having put on the readiness given by the gospel of peace.[8]

This part of our armour is to do with readiness that comes from really living in the gospel of peace. Readiness to go anywhere for the sake of the gospel. If our feet are motivated by the gospel, we will find ourselves in all sorts of interesting situations. These shoes can be quite scary to put on, yet they are an essential part of our armour.

Why do we need shoes to 'stand'? Remember, standing is not passive, we are taking a stand. In the West it is still not so costly to take a stand for the gospel, though there are signs that this is changing. However, some of my friends in Africa and the Middle East pay a great price to stand in gospel shoes.

'D' in the Middle East is a believer from a Christian

---

8. Ephesians 6:15

background with a love for Muslims. He has opened his heart and his home to many Muslims who want to know more about the gospel. As a result he has been arrested, beaten, threatened, and so have many with whom he has worked. His response? To keep on putting those shoes on with the readiness given by the gospel of peace. Paul, who writes to us of this armour, describes himself later in the same chapter as *an ambassador in chains*.[9]

We too must make our stand in these gospel shoes. It may cost us friends, promotion at work, popularity. However, only as we wear them will we be able to make an impact on those around us. This gospel of peace seems to bring such division. Yet, what it really divides is light from darkness.

*But now in Christ Jesus you who once were far off have been brought near by the blood of Christ. For **he himself is our peace**, who has made us both one and has broken down in his flesh the dividing wall of hostility by abolishing the law of commandments expressed in ordinances, that he might create in himself one new man in place of the two, so making peace, and might reconcile us both to God in one body through the cross, thereby killing the hostility.*[10]

Jesus became the gospel (the good news) and became our peace. He did it by violence. By breaking down ***the***

---

9. Ephesians 6:20

10. Ephesians 2:13-16, emphasis added

dividing wall between God and people and between people themselves. That dividing wall was that we had not kept *the law of commandments expressed in ordinances.* Therefore sin stood between us and God, and between us and each other.

The weapon that Jesus brought against this wall of hostility was His own sinless body. He took our punishment, the full weight of the written commandments against us. He carried them into the grave, and there they stay! When He rose from the dead, there was no stain upon Him.

And so, He became our gospel and our peace. Not only did He make us one with Him, but He gave us the possibility to be one with each other no matter what had divided us before. There was answer now for any and every kind of hostility. It is impossible to walk in these shoes if we walk in bitterness or unforgiveness towards each other.

Again we discover that this piece of the armour too is Jesus Himself.

The shield of faith

In all circumstances take up the shield of faith, with which you can extinguish all the flaming darts of the evil one.[11]

How easy it sounds, but how hard at times to find that

---

11. Ephesians 6:16

shield when the arrows are flying. We take a stand over something and it can seem like all hell breaks loose. One of our Board members at the beginning of what is now World Horizons was a man called Ernest Whitehouse. He was the husband of Mary Whitehouse who, throughout the 1960s and 1970s, campaigned particularly against the BBC for broadcasting programmes with bad language and sexually explicit content.

The couple came under constant abuse and attack from many directions. Someone even chose to commit suicide by lying down in a small country lane near where they lived, knowing that Ernest Whitehouse would be driving that way. It was only by constantly raising the shield of faith that they were able to stand.

Faith is a gift[12], and yet the disciples were often rebuked for their lack of it. Does that seem fair? It can only be fair if the gift was already given but somehow not utilised. Jesus said that a mustard seed of faith could move a mountain. My faith does not usually seem to be the mountain moving kind, and yet, would Jesus really have given me less than a mustard seed's worth?

If our God is as generous as we know Him to be, there must be something else going on. Faith is described as a shield. A shield only does what it is designed for when we enter the battle. Could it be that we do not see things change

---

12. Ephesians 2:8

at times because we don't really enter the battle? I find that I can easily get lulled into 'being realistic'. I become weary of taking a stand for healing. I lower my expectations a little about my longing for transformation in my community. My heart gets a little more hardened to the plight of refugees. I am not so expectant of when the next person will get saved.

I need to be stirred again! Woken up. Faith works when it is put into action. The arrows of realism cannot get past the shield of faith when it is raised! There is a greater reality out there; it is called the kingdom of God. Faith grows as it is used and we can overcome bigger obstacles, and see greater miracles, as we continue to stand.

To stand and ***having done all, stand,*** is costly. It is not comfortable. It means that we must stay alert, stirring up our spirit, and continually asking for an infilling of the wonderful Holy Spirit. We cannot do it in our own strength. In fact we must die. Paul found the secret:

> *I have been crucified with Christ. It is no longer I who live, but Christ who lives in me. And the life I now live in the flesh I live by faith in the Son of God, who loved me and gave himself for me.*[13]

No one can truly stand in the face of the enemy's onslaught except the Messiah Himself. In Gethsemane, despite His urging, the disciples all fell asleep. The battle was intense. Jesus stood on His own against the forces of

---

13. Galatians 2:20

darkness, agonising in all of His humanity until He was totally surrendered to the Father's will.

? Jesus love for God

Jesus' faith <u>enabled</u> Him to stand in that garden. That stand led Him to the place of submission even to death on a cross. We will exhaust ourselves with effort that cannot possibly succeed until we learn to do the same. Our strength can only hinder us; it must go to the cross.

Our shield of faith is the same shield the Son of God lifted up, a total submission to the Father's will. It is saying, whatever I am feeling, whatever the circumstances: *I trust You. So I must wake myself up to battle, but that battle is won by surrender.*

The King James version of Galatians 2:20 reads:
*I am crucified with Christ: nevertheless I live; yet not I, but Christ liveth in me: and the life which I now live in the flesh **I live by the faith of the Son of God**, who loved me, and gave himself for me.*[14]

Jesus truly shares Himself with us. He opens His heart and invites us to share the same faith that He has in His heavenly Father. He is our shield!

The helmet of salvation

(A)nd take the helmet of salvation [15]

---

14. Galatians 2:20, KJV, emphasis added
15. Ephesians 6:17

Our crowning glory is Jesus' greatest gift: His life. He crowns our heads with His salvation. Our only obligation is to keep it there, on our heads, covering and renewing our minds. He calls us to live aware of our salvation. God is for us, who can be against us? Who can separate us from the love of God in Christ Jesus? Yet separation can come - or at least perceived separation - not because of any enemy, but through our own thoughts.

In winning our salvation, Jesus also disarmed all of Satan's hordes:

And you, who were dead in your trespasses and the uncircumcision of your flesh, God made alive together with him, having forgiven us all our trespasses, by cancelling the record of debt that stood against us with its legal demands. This he set aside, nailing it to the cross. **He disarmed the rulers and authorities and put them to open shame, by triumphing over them in him.**[16]

So then, Satan has no weapon to use against us. As we saw in the previous chapter, the only thing he can do is to lie. His lies will find a landing place if we allow bitterness or unforgiveness to fester in our minds. If we forget who we are - that we are loved and called and chosen by God - the enemy will burrow into our thoughts, delighting to tell us how useless and powerless we are.

---

16. Clolssians 2:13-15, emphasis added

Our words have power too! I can talk myself into exhaustion when I keep proclaiming how tired I feel. Even this world's medical community realises the strong link between the mind and the body.

How much more is the link between mind and spirit. If I continually think of myself as a failure, I crush my own spirit with the lie that I believe. That thought becomes a stronghold in my mind, so that no matter how many times I succeed, or how much others encourage me, I cannot accept the truth. I have built what Paul called *a lofty opinion raised against the knowledge of God:*

For the weapons of our warfare are not of the flesh but have divine power to destroy strongholds. We destroy arguments and every lofty opinion raised against the knowledge of God, and take every thought captive to obey Christ.[17]

I may think that I am being humble, that I have a right view of myself, but if it is not the way God sees me, it is my own lofty opinion.

Satan will always try to use our own thoughts against us, and add his own brand of deceit to bring us into anger or depression. Sin starts with a thought. Our minds become battlegrounds if we do not keep the helmet of Christ's free gift of salvation on our heads.

---

17. 2 Corinthians 10:4-5

Thank God that the weapons He has given us have His divine power to demolish strongholds!

We wear our helmet by consciously living in the good of the salvation that has been won for us. When we are aware of our salvation, the lies of the enemy cannot control our mind. Every slip we make, we get right with God and with each other, and condemnation cannot find a landing strip.

Jesus' very name means salvation. He Himself is our helmet. As we are clothed in Him we can stand. If we will put on this helmet we will have, as Paul discovered, *the mind of Christ.*[18]

The sword of the Spirit

(T)he sword of the Spirit, which is the word of God, praying[19]

I have taken the liberty to creep into the next verse and add the word *praying* to the weapon that the Lord has given us. Remember the original text did not have verses or punctuation as we know it, so it could just as easily have been read without the comma.

This sword gives such a power to our prayer. Whenever you don't know how to pray, pray the word of God! How wonderful it is to put our names, or those for whom we are

---

18. 1 Corinthians 2:16

19. Ephesians 6:17-18

burdened, into the blessings of God's word. For example:

> *Blessed be the God and Father of our Lord Jesus Christ, who has blessed **Gail** in Christ with every spiritual blessing in the heavenly places, even as he chose **Gail** in him before the foundation of the world, that **she** should be holy and blameless before him. In love he predestined **her** for adoption to himself as **a daughter** through Jesus Christ, according to the purpose of his will.*[20]

Truth is our weapon. It feeds our own souls and enables us to stand.

When there is a specific word breathed to you by the Holy Spirit, there is nothing in this world or in the heavenly realms that can stop it from being fulfilled. Nothing, that is, except us ourselves. The Scripture tells us:

> *"For as the rain and the snow come down from heaven*
> *and do not return there but water the earth,*
> *making it bring forth and sprout,*
> *giving seed to the sower and bread to the eater,*
> *so shall my word be that goes out from my mouth;*
> ***it shall not return to me empty,***
> *but it shall accomplish that which I purpose,*
> *and shall succeed in the thing for which I sent it".*[21]

---

20. Ephesians 1:3-5, personalised
21. Isaiah 55:10-11, emphasis added

The word that God speaks will not return to Him empty. However, there are many words that He has given, promises that He has made, that have never been activated, never been *returned* to Him.

How do we return a word from the Lord? We speak it out, we declare it, we pray it, we obey it. God's word is activated in us by our faith. The sword of the Spirit is the word of God on our lips. That word is part of the One who is the Word, Christ Himself.

The armour of God

So we are invited to put on the whole armour of God so that we can stand in the evil day. Every part of the armour is an aspect of our Messiah. Paul summarised this teaching in his letter to the Romans like this: *But put on the Lord Jesus Christ, and make no provision for the flesh, to gratify its desires.*[22]

We are invited to clothe ourselves with Jesus. He is in us, and He wants us to be in Him, to stand in Him, so that we can fulfil our part as His beloved warriors.

Having done all

A few years ago we realised that to continue to grow the ministry of **Nations** in helping to birth and nurture new mission movements, we needed accommodation for the

---

22. Romans 13:14

young people who were training with those movements. Up until then, they had rented houses in the town. However, contracts were becoming harder to make. Understandably landlords were asking for longer terms than we were able to agree.

For a long time we had prayed over extending our existing premises, but there had been no breakthrough in terms of finance coming in to make it happen. Then the daughter of one of our members told us about an old nursing home that had come onto the market. It was a few minutes' walk from our centre and had 20 bedrooms, all with their own basins, as well as a good-sized kitchen and meeting/dining room.

When we went to look around it, we were all convinced that this would be ideal for us. We discovered that there were at least two other interested parties, and that the sale would be completed by each party presenting a closed offer of what they were willing to pay.

We had a few thousand pounds, but nothing like the money we needed to put in a reasonable offer. Any offer we made had to be backed up with proof that we had the finance. It seemed like an impossible situation, but we felt that the Lord was encouraging us to take this building for Him. God gave us the same word that He told the disciples when he sent them ahead of him to look for a donkey: *"The Lord has need of it".*[23]

---

23. Mark 11:3

So we prayed. The mission movements with which we were working stood united with us. It was their inheritance too! We stood on God's word. As we were praying someone read this parable:

And he said to them, "Which of you who has a friend will go to him at midnight and say to him, 'Friend, lend me three loaves, for a friend of mine has arrived on a journey, and I have nothing to set before him'".[24]

Jesus went on to say that the friend was not happy at first to get out of bed and give him the loaves, but because he persisted, the friend eventually did.

We felt like the man who had friends turning up with nothing to set before them. Young people were coming; they needed somewhere to live. So the Lord encouraged us to go to our friends and ask them to help us. However, we felt we could not ask others to give unless we ourselves had given all that we could.

We took offerings amongst ourselves. Young people from the different teams gave all that they could. A couple sold some land. We emptied our bank accounts, we sold things, we did everything within our power.

Then gifts started to come in from friends. Some offered interest-free loans. We were praying about the amount we

---

24. Luke 11:5-6

should offer. One of the young people had a figure in his heart and eventually worked up the nerve to speak it out. We all witnessed with it.

We were still nearly £100,000 short of what we felt we needed. The deadline to make an offer was drawing near. With a heavy heart I went to the bank to look at the possibility of a mortgage. We did not want to go that way, because we knew that the people coming would not be able to afford any more than we would need to keep the property running. However, it seemed to be the only option.

Incredibly the bank agreed to a mortgage, and so we put in our offer. I had told the bank that we expected more money to come in, so that we would not need the mortgage to be as large as we agreed, but for the sake of the offer, we needed proof that we could pay the money.

Money continued to flow in and I rang the bank manager to lower the mortgage to £80,000. We continued to cry out to the Lord to deliver us from needing a mortgage. One Thursday, during our weekly prayer day, two men from the USA joined us. They were friends of one of our mission leaders.

At the end of the meeting one of them asked us how much the mortgage was. He then offered to cover it! We had no idea that he was the owner of a chain of restaurants in the USA, and was able to completely pay off our mortgage before it had even started!

Amazing! All this happened in a few short weeks. However, that wasn't the end. When the closed offers were revealed, we found that ours was the lowest, so it seemed that there was no way we could get the building. I was in Korea at the time, and remember looking at the email in disbelief. How could we have come so far, and got things so wrong?

I just couldn't accept that the building would go to someone else. When I got back to Wales, I discovered that others felt the same. It seemed absolutely crazy, but we continued to pray for the building to come to us. We explored all possible avenues, but there was no way, humanly speaking, that we could righteously take hold of the building. All we could do was stand on the word that the Lord had given us.

I remember standing outside the building for several mornings in the early hours and shouting (quietly, for fear of waking the neighbours), "Let God arise!" It was over to the Lord. We had done all we knew how to do, and now we could only stand, and wait for Him to act.

Within a couple of weeks we heard that the sale had fallen through! Amazing! Wonderful, but there was still another party ahead of us. We were not allowed to know who the other interested parties were, but somehow word leaked to some of the residents local to 'our' building.

They found out that the party now in line to buy the building was a government funded group which worked with newly released prisoners. Usually these next stage housing projects were smaller properties. However, for some reason they now had their sights on this 20-bedroom place.

We started to pray for the right place for this group. The residents took things into their own hands and staged a sit in, closing the road. The local paper came and took pictures as they sat and waved banners, the most prominent of them reading 'Missionaries, not miscreants!'

Due to the pressure the buyers pulled out, and the building was offered to us! As you may imagine, there was great celebration! God had done something wonderful for us but, more precious still, He had done something special among us. All of us had stood together on His word. All of us experienced the joy of the miracle, and the power of unity in the Spirit. We had learnt together: those barely saved and those who had been with the Lord for many years. All of us had a testimony, and the work had a firm foundation on which to grow.

God given

Chapter 8
Persevering in the Beloved Warrior

Come out! Come out of darkness and the tomb
The life you live, it is not life at all.
I know the fear that grips you seems so strong
Yet, don't you hear that calm, persistent call?

You're tired and cannot face reality,
The lies you're fed wrap tight around your soul.
You feel alone, deserted and unloved,
"If onlys" rise and life has lost its goal.

See through the gloom a man who quietly weeps,
His heart is pierced because He sees your pain
He stretches out His hands, looks straight at you
And with authority calls out your name.

Come as you are, ignore the clinging doubts
They are the grave clothes friends will take away.
"Come out, come out!" it is the call of love
Will you choose life or death, the night, or day?

I see His tears, I hear His voice.
He calls my name, I have a choice.
The daylight hurts, it sears my eyes
Yet I'll no longer live in lies.
His voice so still and yet so strong
Sounds through my soul, O Lord, I come.

Maybe we have all been there? That dark place where it seems that even in our desperation, the Lord has ignored our cries. Prayer is unanswered, tragedy has struck. We are drawn into a cave of helplessness. That is when we need perseverance.

Mary and Martha, and Lazarus himself, must have felt that desperation. They had depended on Jesus, knowing that He loved them, knowing that He was the healer, yet He didn't come. There are many similar accounts in the Scriptures. David was, at one time, so in fear for his life that he had to pretend to be a madman. Gideon and the nation of Israel spent years watching the enemy eat their crops whilst they themselves nearly starved. Anna spent 84 years as a widow worshipping and praying in the temple, waiting and waiting for the Messiah.

Why does God make us wait? Why does He desire perseverance? There are many answers to that question, but an overriding one is what Paul has discovered in the passage below:

Not only so, but we also glory in our sufferings, because we know that suffering produces perseverance; perseverance, character; and character, hope. And hope does not put us to shame, because God's love has been poured out into our hearts through the Holy Spirit, who has been given to us.[1]

What a strange progression. We cannot avoid suffering in this fallen world, but only a loving God could design it so that suffering would actually build us up in the end. Here we see that perseverance in suffering leads to a building of our character, which in turn enables us to hope in situations that seem hopeless. This hope is not some nebulous dream, but something that has its anchor in the certainty of God's love for us.

Jesus is training us to rule and reign with Him for eternity. Our character is something that will travel with us into that realm. It is precious to the Lord, so He refines it.

Now if anyone builds on the foundation with gold, silver, precious stones, wood, hay, straw - each one's work will become manifest, for the Day will disclose it, because it will be revealed by fire, and the fire will test what sort of work each one has done.[2]

Perseverance is a quality of the character of Jesus. He lived

---

1. Romans 5:3-5, NIV

2. 1 Corinthians 3:12-13

for 30 years, knowing who He was, yet quietly waiting for His time to come. He continued making furniture for people while He watched the suffering around Him. He waited, trusting His heavenly Father's timing, despite knowing that the fate of the world was literally in His hands.

If you are anything like me, one of the hardest things to understand is God's timing. So often I have heard correctly, but I jump into 'doing' mode before I have understood the 'wait' of preparation.

That 'wait' can be necessary for many reasons. Every 'wait' when we are waiting on the Lord develops our character, but there are also other more specific reasons.

Hannah

Remember Hannah who so desperately wanted a son? She prayed year by year with tears and great longing. Still the Lord did not answer her. What Hannah did not realise was that her prayers were also a reflection of God's own longing. He too was longing for a 'son'. Someone who would listen to Him and bring Israel out of the time when everyone did what was right in their own eyes, to a time when they would begin to fulfil their destiny to reflect the kingdom of heaven on earth.

Hannah's prayer was for many years totally self-absorbed. She was only looking at her own needs. Then at some point she saw the bigger picture; she began to understand that the

Lord too needed a son.

> *"O Lord of hosts, if you will indeed look on the affliction of your servant and remember me and not forget your servant, but will give to your servant a son, then I will give him to the Lord all the days of his life, and no razor shall touch his head."* [3]

The Lord was waiting patiently for her, as Hannah thought she was waiting for Him! He was opening her heart to understand more of His heart. Eventually Hannah allowed Him to hone her prayer, which was the right prayer. She submitted to Him, cutting out the selfishness.

God is our Father, and when we are young in Him, we cry out and He answers our needs. Yet He doesn't want us to stay as babies, living on the milk of His goodness. He wants to train us to eat meat, to be fit to rule with Him. So He will hold His hand back at times. He does not want a selfish bride, but one who loves Him above herself, and puts His needs above her own.

When Hannah made that heart-rending sacrifice of leaving Samuel in the temple of the Lord, she was filled with supernatural joy, and she sang out a prophecy. In it she 'saw' the king of Israel, and she is the first in all of Scripture to use the word Messiah (anointed one). She saw a glimpse of the fullness of the Son that God would ultimately use to bring not

---

3. 1 Samuel 1:11

only Israel, but all the nations of the world back to Him:

> *"The Lord will judge the ends of the earth;*
> *he will give strength to his king*
> *and exalt the horn of **his anointed**".*[4]

The Lord did not forget Hannah. He gave her three more sons and two daughters. God is no man's debtor! Amen.

It is never a bad idea, when our prayer doesn't seem to get an answer, to test it and see if we are praying out of selfish desires.

Daniel

Sometimes our waiting is necessary because God is working out His larger purposes. This can be very confusing until we realise what is happening. Daniel was a man who loved God even though he was living in an empire that was totally pagan. As a young man he had been dragged from his home and probably castrated. He had lost everything most young men dream of. Yet he stayed faithful to the Lord.

He spent 70 years worshipping God and waiting for His timing. During that time he experienced terrible persecution, but also promotion and favour. At a certain moment while he was reading Jeremiah's prophecy, he realised that God had ordained 70 years of punishment for Israel's disobedience,

---

4. 1 Samuel 2:10, emphasis added

and that the time of deliverance was drawing near.[5] Prayer for deliverance before that time was not unanswered, it just was waiting for God's wider purpose to work out.

Once Daniel had uncovered the promise, he did not just wait for God to act. He understood that God works through His people. He started to fast and pray and repent on behalf of his nation. He completely identified with the sin that had caused his nation to be taken into exile. He knew that however righteous he was, he could never satisfy the righteousness of God. It was only mercy that could save them.

Daniel sought to understand God's heart, and the Lord honoured his request. He not only spoke of the deliverance of Israel, but showed Daniel things that, thousands of years later, are still to be worked out in the end times. That is some prophetic gift! He was able to receive that gift because he persevered. He allowed his character to be formed in the furnace of God's love for him.

God's wider purpose is not just played out on earth, but in the heavenly realms. It is clear from the book of Daniel that there is a battle going on in the heavenly realms. As the apostle Paul later writes, there are princes and powers of darkness.[6] These entities hold nations under their influence.

Once Daniel set himself to pray and fast for 21 days.

---

5. Daniel 9:2

6. Ephesians 6

It seems that through all that time he did not receive any breakthrough. The heavens were like brass. Yet he continued to seek God until an angel appeared to him.

> *"Fear not, Daniel, for from the first day that you set your heart to understand and humbled yourself before your God, your words have been heard, and I have come because of your words."* [7]

It is so encouraging to know that our prayers are always heard, and that they will always have an effect in heaven, even when we feel nothing.

The angel told Daniel that the reason for delayed answer was that he had been withstood by ***the prince of the kingdom of Persia***[8] for 21 days. He also said that the next power to arise and contest him would be ***the prince of Greece, but that Michael***, Israel's prince stood with him.[9]

It cannot be a coincidence that Daniel was at that time under the earthly authority of a Persian king who was later to decree permission for the end of the exile of the Israelites, and their return to Jerusalem! Daniel's prayer had caused the prince of darkness - who had held Persia - to be defeated, so that the Persian king could hear and respond to the call of God! The next kingdom to arise to prominence would be

---

7. Daniel 10:12
8. Daniel 10:13
9. Daniel 10:20-21

Greece. Did the Lord ever find another 'Daniel' to persevere in prayer until that prince was defeated?

We cannot understand all the battle that goes on in the heavenly places, but we do need to know that there are spiritual powers behind earthly authority, and that our prayers effect changes according to God's design.

When we are involved in prayer to do with nations and kingdoms (and the Lord invites us into this battle if we will allow Him to train us in the smaller battles), perseverance is vital. Powers that we do not see are being shifted by our prayer.

Jonathan

Perseverance is necessary, but to have it we must overcome discouragement.

Discouragement is one of the most effective weapons in Satan's arsenal of lies. It literally tries to rob us of our courage. If he can get us to believe that *'It is all too much for me'* or *'Everything I touch goes wrong'*, he has won the battle. Failure is something all of us face at one time or another. It is bitter, and yet it can either be a spur to keep going, or a reason to quit, depending on our mindset. Psalm 46 is a well-known battle song. Towards the end are these famous words:

"Be still, and know that I am God.
I will be exalted among the nations,

I will be exalted in the earth!" [10]

When everything is raging around us, be still and just know that God is in control, and He will be exalted. Yet that word ***still can also be translated fail. Fail and know that I am God!*** His purposes are not affected by our failure. He has made room for us to fail, and still loves us and chooses to use us!

Jonathan had the right attitude to failure. He had really messed up. In his zeal he attacked a Philistine garrison, and in doing so provoked a war that Israel lost.[11] Of course his father Saul went on to make a series of disastrous decisions, but the catalyst was Jonathan. The result of that defeat was that the Philistines took away all the weapons of Israel's army. The only people in Israel who had a sword or a spear were Jonathan and Saul.

The Israelites were humiliated to such an extent that they had to go and pay the Philistines to even sharpen their axes or their ploughshares. The Philistines would allow them no blacksmiths of their own.

I am sure that Jonathan felt awful. Yet he did not allow discouragement and failure to dominate his thoughts. He fixed his eyes on his covenant keeping God. He was not sure if the Lord would use him, but he was prepared to put his life on the line to see! What he did know is that God would save Israel. Listen to what he said to his armour bearer:

---

10. Psalm 46:10
11. 1 Samuel 13

"Come, let us go over to the garrison of these uncircumcised. It may be that the Lord will work for us, for nothing can hinder the Lord from saving by many or by few".[12]

In declaring that the Philistines were **uncircumcised** he was declaring that they were not in covenant with God, and therefore could not stand against those who were. Jonathan and his armour bearer went on to defeat around 20 men, and that defeat sent the Philistines into panic and led to Israel winning a great victory.

Next time we feel discouraged let's remember that we may fail, but when we do, let's be still and know that the Lord is God, and He has not given up on us!

Pearls

Have you ever wondered why the gates of the new Jerusalem are made of pearls? A pearl is formed when a parasite invades an oyster. The oyster is irritated and clothes the parasite with a mantle of nacre again and again. Three or four layers are added each day. If a pearl is only made of a few hundred layers, it can be easily crushed. A quality pearl will have thousands of layers of nacre, representing years of quiet perseverance on behalf of the oyster. The gates of Jerusalem are a lesson to us that we need to persevere.

---

12. 1 Samuel 14:6

Our lives are often invaded by 'parasites': family troubles, attacks from the enemy, consequences of our sin or someone else's sin towards us, illness, loneliness, lack of finances... so many things invade our shells! What can we do? How do we turn trouble into treasure? It has to be by perseverance. Each day fixing our eyes on Jesus. Each day choosing not to give up.

"Is anyone among you suffering? Let him pray." [13]
"Do not be anxious about anything, but in everything by prayer and supplication with thanksgiving let your requests be made known to God." [14]

Don't worry, pray! The parasite can become a pearl! Prayer is like the layer of nacre that the oyster puts over the parasite. The more layers of prayer, the less the situation irritates us, and the more it can be used to bring glory to God. A true pearl has a kind of inner light. The Lord wants to create treasure in our lives.

We may be helpless, but we need never be hopeless, because Jesus took all the parasites of sin and death into His own body on the cross. He did not push them away, but willingly took them into Himself so that He could overcome them by His obedient perseverance. He, unlike any of us, had the power over exactly when and where He would die. Speaking of His life as the good shepherd, Jesus said,

---

13. James 5:13
14. Philippians 4:6

"No one takes it from me, but I lay it down of my own accord. I have authority to lay it down, and I have authority to take it up again. This charge I have received from my Father".[15]

He persevered through those six hours of unimaginable agony on the cross. Not only the physical torture, but the spiritual torment of becoming filthy sin for us, and knowing separation for the first and only time from His Father. He knew exactly when the work had been completed and then, and only then, did He yield His Spirit up to His Father.

He bought for us the pearl of greatest price, our salvation. He is the ultimate model of victorious perseverance. As we stand in Him, we ourselves can persevere.

Twisted bodies

I don't know if you have ever seen the effects of polio? It is a disease that has now largely been eradicated. At the time of writing, there remain just three countries where it still prevails. In the 1980s though, the nation in which I worked was polio's third largest stronghold. It is a cruel disease. If it doesn't kill, it twists the bodies of its victims, often adding them to the ragged swell of beggars on the streets.

Groups of students would come and visit us each summer. Some of these were medical students. As part of their training

---

15. John 10:18

they were able to do an elective in a different part of the world. One of them, let's call her Rachel, asked us if we had any medical contacts. So we began to pray. We visited a number of hospitals, but none seemed interested in receiving elective students. One day, a friend and I were walking through the city asking the Lord to open a door for us, and my friend pointed down a back street. She just felt a prompting to go down a certain alley. Amazingly, we soon found a sign for a hospital we had no idea existed.

As we approached, a doctor was just leaving. We told him what we were looking for, and he was very open. He told us that he was an orthopaedic paediatrician: a bone doctor for children (to the uninitiated, as I was). His heart was breaking because of the number of operations he had to do on kids who were deformed through polio. He knew very well that there was a vaccine, and in fact a lot of the children who fell ill told him that they had been vaccinated, but for whatever reason it was not effective.

Rachel spent a few weeks with him, and was very moved by what she saw. She determined to return and work from the UK to see what could be done. She built up a team of fellow students and friends in medicine, statistics and biomedical sciences, logistics and mechanics to research why these children were still getting polio. It seemed an impossible task: getting ethics permissions, talking to experts, gaining funding, designing questionnaires and consent forms in three languages. When they began they were all only students.

Rachel kept up with the doctor by regular visits, sometimes taking new colleagues. They then found out that a major children's development charity had tried to do similar research, and hadn't been able to get government approval. On top of that they heard that the World Health Organisation (WHO) was being told that the country had 'no problem' with polio.

This testimony is not of my perseverance but that of Rachel and the team. Despite all the obstacles, they were determined to find out why the polio vaccines were not effective. Rachel was told that what was needed was a serum antibody study of the blood of children who had been vaccinated. They would also have to find an accredited medical organisation to analyse the blood, which would be expensive.

Amazingly she found an official institute in London which was not only willing to analyse the blood, but would pay all the transportation costs and provide much needed field equipment. The institute was keen to help because it was in the middle of a worldwide research project into polio!

It took a couple of years of prayer and preparation, but eventually everything was in place and the team of volunteers was ready to go. People freely gave months of their time to make this project work. The orthopaedic paediatrician, we will call him Dr A, helped them to get the equipment into the country. However, when they arrived he told them that to conduct the research they needed to get permission for the project from the Ministry of Health. This is what others had tried and failed to do. It was a daunting prospect.

Dr A wrote a letter of introduction to the Minister of Health. The team also wrote, but did not hear anything from the Ministry. They decided to just go to the office and wait until they were granted an appointment. It could have been a very long wait, but two things were in their favour. Firstly, Dr A was known to the Ministry because he was one of the doctors to the royal family. Secondly, on a previous visit to the city some of the team had met a lovely lady in an ex-patriot church, who turned out to be the secretary to the UK ambassador. She was able to secure a letter from the ambassador requesting assistance and safe passage for the team. So after 'only' a two-day wait, they were granted a meeting.

What Rachel did not know was that at the same time she and her team were praying and preparing, UNICEF had quietly approached the Ministry of Health with funding for a mass polio vaccination campaign. However, it said that the funding would only be available if there were some way of evaluating the success of the campaign. The Minister up until that point could not meet the requirements. Rachel stepped into his office at just the right time! Had she gone in a year before, when the project was first trying to get off the ground, it is unlikely that she would have succeeded.

The team she had gathered was hoping to take blood

samples from children from one province of the country, but the Minister asked if they would consider taking them for the whole of the country twice: once before, and once after the national campaign! This was way beyond anything that they had prepared for. In the end they agreed that they could take samples twice from children from three major provinces, giving a good cross section of the whole nation.

The Minister of Health said that the government would provide all the infrastructure and personnel to make things work; all the team had to do was ask for what they wanted! The Institute in London was delighted to be able to get a larger cross section and number of blood samples, and agreed to do all the processing. God had arranged a win-win for everyone in a miraculous alignment of timing.

So with a team of more than 50 national nurses alongside them, in vehicles provided by the government, run on official diesel and with government drivers, this little team of students and newly qualified professionals completed the project within the tight timescale. They stayed in accommodation funded by the Ministry of Health, and even some that was normally reserved for the government or the palace! The King took a personal interest and asked to be kept informed.

The project meant that the team had to visit the same children to take blood before and after they were given the vaccine, to make sure that they were now showing immunity. Usually there was a gap of several months between visits.

One thing that shocked the team was that in the poorer areas some of the children they had tested had died, not of polio, but of starvation before they returned. They realised that so much more is needed in the fight against poverty.

Once the work was done on the ground, and the lab work had been completed, the team then had to begin writing up and analysing its findings. They were all going back to studies or jobs, and doing it largely in their spare time. It seemed that every kind of pressure came on them, or on their families, to delay and try to stop this work from getting finished.

However, when the pressure started to seem unbearable the WHO stepped in and provided funding for one of the team - let's call her Verity - to stop work for a few months, and give herself fully to working on all the statistics. They also sent over an analyst from the USA to assist her. What started with a small team listening to that 'still small voice' was now stirring international attention, with experts, ministers and the King himself pushing to get results.

The analysis was completed and the report was eventually finished. The findings were very helpful to UNICEF, to the WHO and to the country's Ministry of Health. They found that most of the children now had good immunity, but in Dr A's province the gains in immunity were not as strong. The team uncovered that the cold chain (the chain of storage to keep the vaccine live) had been broken. There were not enough fridges, and some were old and ineffective. That was why Dr A had found himself operating on lots of crippled children.

This was easily rectified. The year after the project was completed, polio was completely eradicated from the country! Thousands of healthy children are running around today because a small team persevered. They waited on God's kairos timing; the time that only He knew. In that time God aligned everyone from a King, a Minister and international organisations, to a willing team of believers, with the purposes of heaven. And He answered the cry of a surgeon whose heart was breaking.

Chapter 9
Faithful in the Beloved Warrior

The stars, the sand, a son and sons,
The gospel sounds so strange.
A hope, a prayer, a word, a dream,
My world is rearranged.

A hope against all hope I find,
I know that I will be
The father of the promised child,
Laughter, unfettered, free.

Laughter that rebukes the foe
And shuts the mouths of kings
And dares to ask for nations rule,
And joins with heaven, and sings.

Laughter that makes the water wine,
And makes the crooked straight,
That's pierced and broken, bruised and dies
To open wells of faith.

Laughter that cannot be held
By rock or guard or seal
That rises simply with the dawn
And all that's broken, heals.
In wounded, faltering, fearful hearts
The laugh of faith will come,
As sons and daughters as the sand
From every nation take their stand
Speak hope and healing to the land
And join with Laughter the great plan
And stand and overcome.

It is impossible to separate God from His faithfulness: *if we are faithless, he remains faithful - for he cannot deny himself.*[1]

Our Lord cannot be other than who He is! This is the rock on which we stand; He loves us and He is faithful to us. As we fix our eyes on the Faithful One rather than our challenges, faith will rise in our own hearts too.

In this look at the faithful warrior who fights for us, I am going to use the example that the Bible does: God's faithfulness to the nation of Israel. In Chapter 1 we looked at the covenant of betrothal that Jesus made with us, His bride, when He spoke to His disciples and instigated the communion meal before He went to the cross. This covenant

---

1. 2 Timothy 2:13

was made first to twelve Jewish disciples. The resurrected Jesus commanded them to take the gospel to all nations. Even then they still needed dreams, visions and revelations before they began to realise that this covenant was meant for people from every tribe and nation, not just the Jews.

Nowadays things are reversed. The Gentiles (the nations) hold the gospel as belonging to them. Many have no thought for the original recipients of the covenants and the promises of God. There is ungodly teaching that says that because Jews crucified Jesus and cried out that they and their children would be held accountable for His death,[2] they have forfeited their right to salvation. This teaching undergirded the Holocaust.[3] Jesus' own words from the cross gloriously testify to His heart for the Jews and the Gentiles who were crucifying Him: *"Father, forgive them, for they know not what they do".*[4]

Faith in the Faithful One

God's intention right from the beginning of creation was that people would live by faith. When Adam and Eve ate from the tree of the knowledge of good and evil they rejected faith in favour of their own wisdom. So throughout the generations the Lord sought people who would choose faith. He found people like Enoch, Noah and eventually Abraham who chose to trust Him rather than themselves. With these people the

---

2. Matthew 27:25

3. Read Martin Luther, 'On the Jews and their Lies'

4. Luke 23:34

Lord could build. The gospel was preached to Abraham:

And the Scripture, foreseeing that God would justify the Gentiles by faith, preached the gospel beforehand to Abraham, saying, **"In you shall all the nations be blessed".**[5]

The gospel is inherently good news for every nation. It was God's plan that He would choose one nation to demonstrate His character and purpose, and that through that all the other nations would have the blessing of coming to know Him too. Israel has had times when she successfully fulfilled God's plan, as in the reigns of David and Solomon, and times of abject failure, as Isaiah expresses so vividly:

We were with child, we writhed in labour,
but we gave birth to wind.
We have not brought salvation to the earth,
and the people of the world have not come to life.[6]

The only certain way of the gospel being understood by Israel and all the nations was through the one descendant of Abraham who would be able to walk perfectly in God's plan: God Himself coming as the Son of God and yet the Son of Man.

Jesus' human origin was through the tribe of Judah. He lived as a Jew, under Jewish law, though He marvellously

---

5. Galatians 3:8, emphasis added

6. Isaiah 26:18, NIV

liberated that law from the religious spirit of the Pharisees. He was very clear that His calling was to the lost sheep of Israel[7], but just as clear that the disciples were to take this gospel to all nations. Jesus lived and died a Jew. There is no reason to suppose that He disowned His Jewish identity at the resurrection.

Does Israel have a higher standing in God's sight than any other nation? I don't believe so, but the people of Israel do have a particular calling. They have been chosen by God in fulfilment of promises made to their forefathers Abraham, David and so on. They have been called as a light (to show God and His faithfulness) to the nations.[8] That they have not always fulfilled that calling is obvious, yet **the gifts and the calling of God are irrevocable**.[9]

It was to them that the Lord first gave the Ten Commandments which have become the basis of law in most democracies. It was with them that the Lord first made covenants that Christians throughout the world now enjoy as their own. Those covenants promised many things, but there was a common thread in all of them: descendants and land.

And he brought him outside and said, "Look toward heaven, and number the stars, if you are able to number them". Then he said to him, "So shall your

---

7. Matthew 15:24

8. Isaiah 49:6

9. Romans 11:29

offspring be" ... On that day the Lord made a covenant with Abram, saying, "To your offspring I give this land, from the river of Egypt to the great river, the river Euphrates, the land of the Kenites, the Kenizzites, the Kadmonites, the Hittites, the Perizzites, the Rephaim, the Amorites, the Canaanites, the Girgashites and the Jebusites".[10]

This is God's covenant with Abram. It is very specific regarding the location of the land that the Lord had assigned to his descendants. He confirmed this covenant with Isaac[11] along with a promise that his descendants would bless the nations. When Jacob dreamed at Bethel, the Lord gave this deceitful man who was running for his life the same promise of land and descendants who would bless the nations.[12] This was certainly not a covenant that was dependent on good behaviour.

Unconditional covenant

If we look at the original covenant God made with Abram in Genesis 15, we see that the Lord put Abram into a deep sleep when He spoke to him. God first spoke of how Abram's people would be slaves in Egypt. This is not something that anyone would ever want to hear about their descendants. Yet the Lord knew all that would happen, including the sin of

---

10. Genesis 15:5 & 15:18-21

11. Genesis 26:3-4

12. Genesis 28:13-14

Joseph's brothers to sell him as a slave to Egypt. The covenant did not protect them from the consequences of their sin. Yet, neither did sin stop the covenant from being fulfilled. God then promised to bring them out of slavery with great possessions.

It was after that prophetic revelation that the Lord cut the covenant. Usually a covenant is made between two parties. Abram was told to prepare and cut animals, as was the way when two leaders wanted to make a covenant. The normal practice then would be that each man would walk between the dead animals in a figure of eight. Eight is the number associated with new beginnings. As they walked each would declare the covenant he was making with the other, symbolically saying, 'May I be cut like these animals if I break this covenant'.

This covenant was so important to the Lord that He would not ask a frail man to keep it. So He put Abram to sleep and passed through the animals Himself in two forms, as the flaming torch and the smoking fire pot.[13] He was swearing that the covenant to give the land from the Nile to the Euphrates was unconditional. If He broke His word He would be cut, if Abraham's descendants broke their part by not taking the land, He would be cut also!

It foreshadowed the cross. We were asleep in sin. We could not take our own promised land, but Jesus became the covenant for us. He fulfilled God's part as the Son of

---

13. Genesis 15:17

God, and our part as the Son of Man, by His own obedience and sacrifice. God was cut to enable us to come into our full inheritance. That inheritance will always contain descendants (people who will find salvation because of our testimony and love) and land (physical areas that we can take back, be they houses, streets, towns, cities or even nations as we walk with the Lord in obedience).

How faithful is our God! When we do not remain faithful He still does, because He cannot deny Himself. Our sins will still have consequences in this world, but when we enter into the covenant cut on the cross, there is always redemption for us. He has promised us a hope and a future, and died to make sure that we can access it. This is the way He fights!

However, it is evident that we do not always take the inheritance that Jesus died to give us, just as Israel did not always take the land given to them. That is because as agents of free will, we do not have to accept what the Lord has freely given us.

Consecration

In Genesis 17 the Lord speaks again about this covenant. He invites Abram and Sarai to embrace new names which describe their true destiny as the father and mother of nations. To do this they will need to reject their old nature, which in Genesis 16 had led to them trying to work out God's promises in their own strength, resulting in Ishmael's birth.

The Lord asked that every male would have the covenant

cut in his own flesh. That they would be circumcised. It is a willing cutting of a covenant with the Almighty. The circumcision God wants is of the heart, not just the flesh. If we want to enter into the fullness of our new identity in Christ, and the fullness of the promise for land and spiritual descendants, we must allow His Spirit to cut away our old nature and create a new heart in us. It is our response of faith to our faithful God.

Israel, our model

So, if we study God's dealings with Israel throughout the Scriptures we can also see a model that applies to us. Israel is our older brother; we as individuals, and as nations, all have the same Father. As God is faithful to Israel, so He is faithful to our nation. As God was faithful to Abraham, so He is faithful to us.

As He gives Israel specific land, so He does for each nation.

*And he made from one man every nation of mankind to live on all the face of the earth, **having determined allotted periods and the boundaries of their dwelling place, that they should seek God,** and perhaps feel their way toward him and find him. Yet he is actually not far from each one of us.*[14]

There is something about a people being in the right place

---

14. Acts 17:26-27, emphasis added

that facilitates them seeking God. Satan, feeding on human greed, has fomented wars throughout history to try and prevent this.

As Israel has a particular role, so the Lord also has a specific role or destiny for every tribe and nation. He has gifted nations with certain strengths and characteristics. I know it is not good to stereotype, but it is interesting to see that, like the tribes who came to make David king, each with their offerings and skills[15], there seem to be strengths that the Lord has put within each nation. These strengths can either be used for the kingdom of God or the kingdom of this world.

I work with many Koreans, and have often been blessed by their perseverance, particularly in prayer. I have found that many Egyptians seem to have a deep revelation of the intimate love of God. Maybe it is a heritage from the early Desert Fathers? Some of my Central African friends have seen amazing miracles, including resurrection from the dead. There are Chinese Christian leaders who believe that the Lord has called China specifically to take back the Silk Road, 5,000miles where the gospel has not yet strongly penetrated, leading back to Jerusalem.

Of course we all have access to all the gifts, and the Lord could call us anywhere, whatever our nationality. Yet I find it helpful sometimes to take overviews. The Lord has

---

15. 1 Chronicles 12:23-37

prepared good works for us to do as individuals,[16] could it not also be that He has good works prepared for the church in each nation? If so, to begin to understand this would give us powerful direction in prayer. If national church leaders could sense the calling of the Holy Spirit for their nation, what unity it could inspire! If leaders met together internationally and agreed to share strengths and resources, how quickly would God's kingdom come to earth?

Full salvation

God's faithfulness has given us salvation. Salvation cannot be fully defined in this world. Yet to explore and experience it as much as we can while we are here will lead us to fruitfulness. It is the bare minimum to believe that Jesus died for our sins. That is a glorious truth, but only the starting point of salvation. Jesus Himself said that He would give His life for nothing less than the life of the world.

"(T)he bread that I will give for the life of the world is my flesh." [17]

He came to bring us eternal and full life. This starts the moment we are saved. He told His disciples that they would do the same works as He did, and even greater things.[18] We have examples throughout the ages of men and women who

---

16. Ephesians 2:10
17. John 6:51
18. John 14:12

took Him at His word. They became faithful warriors of the Faithful One. Our challenge is to explore our own salvation in our life on earth, and live it to the full. This gospel that we have been given holds in it the seeds of blessing for every nation. We, as Abraham's offspring, inherit the same promise he received: to be *heirs of the world,*

> *For the promise to Abraham and his offspring that he would be heir of the world did not come through the law but through the righteousness of faith.*[19]

It is the promise of Eden restored. Faith is the key to the blessing of the nations. We often think the answer lies in good government and in flourishing economies, but the baseline is faith. By faith we discover the inheritance the Lord has given us in people and in land. Interestingly the Bible tells us that faith begins with hope.

> *Now faith is the assurance of things hoped for, the conviction of things not seen.*[20]

What are your hopes for yourself, your family, your community, your nation? Those hopes expressed in the presence of the Lord become the prayer that seeds faith.

Replacement?

There is a teaching that says that the church has now

---

19. Romans 4:13

20. Hevrews 11:1

replaced Israel in the covenants that have been made. That because the descendants of Abraham are not just according to the flesh, but according to faith, the promises are not now for those who are merely descendants of the flesh.

The apostle Paul has a lot to say about this misinterpretation in his letter to the Romans.

I ask, then, has God rejected his people? By no means! For I myself am an Israelite, a descendant of Abraham, a member of the tribe of Benjamin. God has not rejected his people whom he foreknew.[21]

If the Lord would 'replace' those to whom He made a promise with others, for whatever reason, that would leave all of us insecure. Either He is faithful or He is not. The Lord does not 'replace', but He does include. He is love, and love by its very nature is inclusive.

So I ask, did they stumble in order that they might fall? By no means! Rather, through their trespass salvation has come to the Gentiles, so as to make Israel jealous. Now if their trespass means riches for the world, and if their failure means riches for the Gentiles, how much more will their full inclusion mean! [22]

The Lord was always working to a plan that would offer salvation to every nation and every individual in the world.

---

21. Romans 11:1-2
22. Romans 11:11-12

His heart is generous. He will not abandon Israel, even though they have largely abandoned Him. It is incredible that wherever they went to in the world, and despite sustained persecution, Jews have held on to their heritage. There has always been a remnant which has tried to keep the commandments and remember the Torah, containing the covenants of God.

The Lord enabled something quite unprecedented in the history of the world. He brought Israel back to the land He had promised them even after 2,000 years of not being known as a nation. As I write, Israel celebrates its 70th year as a restored nation. In this day and age, we are witnessing more Jewish people finding faith in Jesus their Messiah than ever before.

Does that mean that Israel is a holy nation? No. Does it mean that the Lord is pleased with all they do and say? Definitely not! Does it mean that God doesn't love the Palestinians as much as the Israelis? No again! It means that God is faithful. That He has a plan for every people and nation. He has inheritance for Palestinians as well as Israelis. He has land for them and people for them to reach and bless. His heart is broken when bombs go off killing Jews in Israel, and yet His heart is just as broken by the injustices and suffering experienced by people in the West Bank and Gaza.

The Middle East, as one of the great crossroads of the world, is such a mixture of ethnic roots that it may well be that some Palestinians will find that they have Jewish ancestors. The Jews we know of today are largely from the tribes of Benjamin and Judah. There are many theories, some now proven with DNA evidence, of where the other ten tribes are. Let's not forget too that the Lord also blessed Ishmael and multiplied his descendants. He would never have done so if He didn't have an amazing plan for the Arab nations. His desire is that everyone would be saved. He has made faith the great leveller.

The Lord chose to demonstrate His purposes through one nation, so that all nations could learn about Him. That nation of Israel, through its Messiah and through the guarding of the Scriptures, has been a blessing to every other nation on earth. We who are believers have a debt of gratitude to those who, down the millennia, have held what we have come to share:

They are Israelites, and to them belong the adoption, the glory, the covenants, the giving of the law, the worship, and the promises. To them belong the patriarchs, and from their race, according to the flesh, is the Christ, who is God over all, blessed forever. Amen.[23]

End times

The Middle East has always been a flashpoint of war and extremism. Israel, since its rebirth, has been at the centre of

---

23. Romans 9:4-5

the conflict. Surely this is more than merely natural. The Bible speaks through many of its prophets of the final conflict being in the Middle East, and particularly Israel.[24] Jesus Himself warns of the antichrist or the abomination of desolation who will stand in the rebuilt temple. This was partially fulfilled in AD70 when the last temple was destroyed, but points also to the final antichrist:

> *"So when you see the abomination of desolation spoken of by the prophet Daniel, standing in the holy place (let the reader understand), then let those who are in Judea flee to the mountains. Let the one who is on the housetop not go down to take what is in his house, and let the one who is in the field not turn back to take his cloak. And alas for women who are pregnant and for those who are nursing infants in those days! Pray that your flight may not be in winter or on a Sabbath. For then there will be great tribulation, such as has not been from the beginning of the world until now, no, and never will be".*[25]

Antisemitism has a long and ignoble history. The Bible speaks of this growing to such an extent in the final days that all nations will come against Jerusalem.[26] In the same chapter it also speaks of Jesus coming back to the Mount of Olives, and judgement coming on the nations who will not come to

---

24. Ezekiel 38 & 39; Zechariah 14; Revelation 20:7-10

25. Matthew 24:15-21

26. Zechariah 14

Jerusalem to worship at the Feast of Tabernacles (sometimes called the Feast of Booths). This is the final feast of the Jewish calendar biblically, and celebrates the fullness of the harvest. It speaks prophetically about a worldwide harvest of souls.

The last days will be days of conflict for all people. Each person and each nation will have to choose whom they will follow. There will be great destruction and great salvation. Israel, and our attitude towards her, will be at the centre of it all.

Israel is not 'best' among the nations, but she is the 'first', simply because of the fact that the Lord found faith in a man called Abraham. If the Lord could desert her, what confidence would we have that He would not desert us? He is faithful. He asks us to honour His choices. After all, He chose us!

Our faith comes as we realise just how faithful He is. In these tumultuous days, He is our Rock, and on this Rock we take our stand of faith.

Arabs and Jews

I was 20 years old when I met Jesus, and within months He had given me a heart for the Arab nations. Israel was nowhere on my radar. However, a few years later when I was living in an Arab nation, I was struck again and again by Scriptures, some of which I have used in this chapter, that spoke of God's faithfulness to Israel. I spoke to our mission leader about it, and the next time he visited us he brought us some cassette tapes by a friend of his called Lance Lambert. He was a

Messianic Jew living in Jerusalem. Each month he would send out a tape speaking of the present situation in the Middle East, and drawing on the Scriptures to explain prophesy or provoke prayer.

A hope started to grow in my heart that is still with me to this day. It is that there would be a time when Jewish and Arab believers would go out from Israel carrying the gospel to the nations and demonstrating the truth of Ephesians 2:14:

For he himself is our peace, who has made us both one and has broken down in his flesh the dividing wall of hostility.

I travelled to Israel in 1989 with Pam, a friend and colleague who felt that the Lord was calling her there. She was drawn to Haifa, so we spent most of our time in that city. When we spoke to believers in the land, people told us that we had to choose to work with either Jews or Arabs. I am glad to say that is not the case today. In many ministries Jews and Arabs stand side by side for the gospel.

We stayed in a building that was owned by a Christian group, and we heard that the group was looking to sell it. We got the plans of the building and began to ask the Lord if He wanted to establish our work there. As we prayed we felt the Lord telling us that many Christian groups wanted to come and 'plant their flag' in Israel, but He did not want us to do that. He challenged us to pray for a work which was to come.

He began to describe it to us.

Haifa is built on Mount Carmel, and the Lord told us that this coming work would have the spirit and power of Elijah. It would stand uncompromisingly for holiness and would minister to both Jews and Arabs. As part of this prayer, which was to become an intercession, the Lord asked me to stop drinking alcohol, just as He had required of John the Baptist. We knew we were praying for a ministry that would prepare the way of the Lord.

On that same trip we spent a night at the very top of Mount Carmel in a Christian guest house called Stella Carmel. While we were there, the Lord spoke to me very clearly again. He showed me a single poppy growing out of dry ground in the land surrounding the guest house, and said that in this place He would build His church – that it would be a place where Jews and Arabs would worship Him together.

In 1990 Pam and I went back to the first building to pray. By now this building had been bought by a Swiss group which was looking to rent it to Christian and Messianic ministries. While we were there we met a couple from New York who had just made 'aliyah' (literally meaning 'to go up' in Hebrew, it is the term used for Jews returning to live in the land of Israel). Their names were David and Karen Davis. They had been sent out from Times Square Church, David Wilkerson's ministry, and had just started Bible studies with the theme of holiness in that building with Jews and Arabs! They were there because they were looking for a base to start a rehabilitation work for Jewish and Arab men. We arrived the day the Swiss group was going to interview them.

We immediately knew that this was the ministry for which we had been praying. We were able to support them in prayer as they spoke to the Swiss group. They were given a lease on the building, and the place in which the Lord had told me to give up alcohol became House of Victory ('Beit Nitzachon'), a rehabilitation centre for Jews and Arabs with backgrounds of alcohol and drug abuse!

Some time later the Lord showed us a third building, this time in central Haifa. We felt that this too would be part of the ministry. He told us that this building had to do with the nations. My friend and I felt very much that Haifa was a gateway (not just in the natural but in the spiritual realm). We had spent time at the gates of the port proclaiming them open for all whom the Lord wanted to bring in and to send out. He has since brought many Russian Jews in through that gateway, and now Messianic Jews and Christian Arabs are beginning to be sent out in unity as "one new man" with the gospel message, as forerunners of Isaiah's prophecy:

In that day Israel will be the third with Egypt and Assyria, a blessing in the midst of the earth.[27]

---

27. Isaiah 19:24

Present day

David Davis has now gone to be with the Lord, but the ministry he and Karen started is still thriving in the three locations the Lord showed us. Pam worked for about 15 years alongside this ministry.

Their main congregation, Carmel congregation ('Kehilat HaCarmel'), meets in the very place the Lord showed us at the top of Mount Carmel. They were given the land, and built a wonderful sanctuary with twelve stones around the altar, representing the altar that Elijah restored. They proclaim from the very highest place on Carmel the unity of Israel in the living stones of "one new man" - Jew, Arab and Gentile - all of whom are part of the congregation.

The House of Victory is one of the most successful rehabilitation programmes in Israel, and both Jews and Arabs have been transformed through its ministry. The third building the Lord showed us, Beit Yedidia ('House of God's Friend'), was also miraculously given to them. It has become a conference centre and can accommodate up to 90 people. They run several schools of ministry for the nations each year, among other things. They also run a food and clothing programme and a shelter for women and children.

God is faithful, and because of that we too can become faithful warriors. Israel is key to the battle, and I believe that reconciled Jews and Arabs will be absolutely vital to the gospel going out in power in these last days.

Chapter 10
Surrender to the Beloved Warrior

I looked around; a hill to climb,
A cliff to scale, a sea to swim,
A deed to prove my love, my worth,
Oh, that I might just please my King.

I saw the need, the cries, the pain,
And my heart groaned and burned with zeal.
A world of people there to win,
A broken pattern He could heal.

A desperation filled my soul,
Lord use me, take me, show your plan!
And then a vision blazed the trail,
I followed on as lovers can.

But something cracked along the way
Confusion, pain now filled my head
Revealing all that's made of clay
Exposing depths, the great unsaid.

Strange, the kind light here recognised
That I could not have seen before.
The goal is not as I supposed,
My great self-failure is the door.

If only He is satisfied
Success or failure, what are they?
The end is sure, my little part
His treasure in a pot of clay.

It may seem strange to have surrender as the final theme in this book about intimacy and warfare, yet it is the very key that our Beloved Warrior gave us for victory. Surrender in Him and to Him is our ultimate weapon. In fact we cannot surrender to Him unless we surrender in Him. Our fallen human nature seeks self-preservation. We will always avoid the cross until we choose to abide in Him and draw from His nature.

Western Christianity, and therefore what we have exported around the world, is often 'success driven'. We put pressure on ourselves and on each other to produce results. Unwittingly we can easily become motivated by guilt. We feel we never quite measure up to what is expected. We try harder, we fail, we hide our failure because we are afraid of what others will think of us. This leads to stress, depression, deceit. Our very identity comes under attack because we have shifted our gaze from what the Lord thinks about us to what our peers think about us.

Yet Jesus won His battle by what looked like failure to everyone else. The seed falling into the ground and dying never gets the acclaim. It may take three days or three decades, but a seed that holds life from God will always multiply.

The Lord is wanting to free us from the fear of man in all its subtle and acceptable forms. The only way to find this freedom is with a willing surrender to Him. He then becomes the only one whose good opinion we desire. The amazing thing about the fear of the Lord is that it leads us deeper into love with Him. He is not a demanding taskmaster who is seeking results, but a loving Father who is seeking the obedience that comes from devoted children. That obedience in itself leads us into greater freedom, because He knows just who we are and what will utterly fulfil us.

I have found that true surrender comes in stages, and I guess is never totally achieved in this lifetime. When I first met Jesus I gladly surrendered to Him, letting Him take control of my life. I thought I had given Him everything. Yet the more I know Him, the more I see of my selfishness. The more I experience His unconditional love, the more I realise how conditional my love can be.

In this chapter on surrender, I want us to see as clearly as we can the nature of the One to whom we abandon ourselves.

This seeing, this fixing our eyes on the One who is above, will in itself release us into a deeper surrender.

The Lamb reigns

Jesus is the Lamb of God. He rules the universe today as the wounded Lamb on the throne.

> *Then I saw a Lamb, looking as if it had been slain, standing at the centre of the throne, encircled by the four living creatures and the elders. The Lamb had seven horns and seven eyes, which are the seven spirits of God sent out into all the earth.*[1]

Lamb in this passage is used in the diminutive form. Our Lord is described here as the 'little Lamb'. John had been told not to weep because the Lion of the tribe of Judah was coming to open the scroll, but what he saw was the Lamb. The Lion is a lamb! This Lamb has seven horns, perfect strength! Strength that has been made perfect in the 'weakness' of surrender to the Father's will.

A lion comes to rule, a lamb to be sacrificed. Jesus chose to go silently to slaughter so that He would not have to rule as a lion. We have an intercessor before the throne of God whose mercy triumphs over judgement!

So with His warfare, Jesus fights not with the strength of a

---

1. Revelation 5:6, NIV

lion, but through the surrender of a lamb.

They will wage war against the Lamb, but the Lamb will triumph over them because he is Lord of lords and King of kings - and with him will be his called, chosen and faithful followers.[2]

In this time of turmoil and shaking, the Lamb is calling His army to Himself; his chosen and

faithful followers. He is inviting us to fight with His beautiful weapons, the fruit of the Spirit: **love, joy, peace, patience, kindness, goodness, faithfulness, gentleness and self-control.**[3] No law can touch these things and Satan cannot comprehend them. The world cannot defeat them. We fight in the strength of weakness. We win by losing and live by dying.

To live in daily surrender as a 'lamb' there are some very practical steps we can take.

Forgiveness

Forgiveness undergirds this call to be like a lamb. We cannot stand, we cannot pray in truth unless we are walking in forgiveness. That means that we also need to forgive ourselves.

There is a power in forgiveness that can melt the hardest

---

2. Revelation 17:14, NIV

3. Galatians 5:22-23

heart. Saul, who was to become the apostle Paul, stood and watched Stephen being stoned to death. He wholeheartedly approved of what was happening, as the witnesses against Stephen had laid their garments at his feet whilst they got on with the gruesome job. He heard Stephen pray for the forgiveness of his persecutors with the agony of his dying breath.[4]

There was no immediate transformation; Saul went on to ravage the church, and probably witnessed again and again the peace the believers had, and the forgiveness flowing from them. Yet with time all he saw must have disrupted his heart and prepared him for his meeting with the risen Jesus on the road to Damascus.

Of course forgiveness doesn't always 'work'. The centurion crucifying Jesus may have found faith, but there were plenty around that day who did not. And that is maybe the hardest thing. We must forgive where it is least deserved, with no expectation that it will even make a difference to that person's life or behaviour. It is an act of love and like any act of love, it may not be received. However, love released will always have an impact somewhere.

Jesus wants to bring us to the place where we accept the wounds that others give us, and allow them to go free, longing for their blessing, even if they never receive it. We too are called to rule as He does, as wounded lambs.

---

4. Acts 7:60

Forgiveness is the most unnatural act to our human nature. Yet when it is demonstrated it brings the power of the cross into our everyday situations. It is an act of intercession. It is love in action.

Laying down a heavy yoke of bitterness, or even our own version of 'righteous anger', can be hard. When we have been abused and mistreated, and continue to be so, it seems almost impossible to let go of our right to 'justice'.

The world is growing more and more polarised. How can Arab forgive Jew, or Jew Arab? There is so much blood between them. Can the Rohingya ever love the people of Myanmar, or the Yazidis be reconciled with ISIS fighters? Something beyond the roar of a lion, far greater than military might or great intellect is needed.

Jesus lived the way. The way of the Lamb.

Gentleness and humility

The only way the King of the universe ever described His heart was gentle and humble. It is the heart of the Lamb.

"Take my yoke upon you and learn from me, for I am gentle and humble in heart, and you will find rest for your souls." [5]

---

5. Matthew 11:29, NIV

Jesus makes it clear that we are to learn from Him. He is not a far-off commander who simply gives orders; His humility and gentleness have brought Him near to us and made Him approachable for us, even in the depths of our sin. Yet this same gentleness and humility defeated all the powers of hell.

Jesus knew that it was the only way to freedom. Humility and gentleness are places free from anxiety; places of rest. The humble heart does not have anything to prove. It does not have to fight for position or recognition. It says, *I know who I am, and God knows who I am. That is enough.*

The Beatitudes better than anything else show this humble, gentle heart of Jesus. The Jews of His day had made the Ten Commandments into a religious race for righteousness. They had twisted them and added to them until they tied the common people in knots, while their leaders boasted in their right standing with God.

Jesus upheld the law, but also spoke of its spirit, unmasking the hypocrisy around Him. The ones God favours are not the religious leaders, but those who are poor in spirit and in worldly wealth. The meek, those hungering for true righteousness, the mourners, and the persecuted are blessed! Anger is a kind of murder, lust is the same as adultery and enemies are to be loved.

This is not the teaching of the Lion, but of the Lamb of God. Jesus in this teaching is showing us His own nature: *poor, mourning, hungering, meek, pure, persecuted, peacemaking.*[6] He invites us to follow Him into this strange and blessed life that so disrupts the wisdom of this world.

The wounds of love

On the day of His resurrection Jesus commissioned the disciples to go out into the world as He had done, like a lamb. There is nothing more glorious and more definitive in victory than the resurrection. Yet there was none of the usual conquerors' attitude in Jesus. He is more than a conqueror! He didn't stand in the temple and demand the people repent and worship Him. He taught His followers humility.

> *On the evening of that day, the first day of the week, the doors being locked where the disciples were for fear of the Jews, Jesus came and stood among them and said to them, "Peace be with you". When he had said this, he showed them his hands and his side. Then the disciples were glad when they saw the Lord. Jesus said to them again, "Peace be with you. As the Father has sent me, even so I am sending you". And when he had said this, he breathed on them and said to them, "Receive the Holy Spirit. If you forgive the sins of any, they are forgiven them; if you withhold forgiveness from any, it is withheld".*[7]

---

6. Matthew 5:1-12

7. John 20:19-23

Jesus showed His disciples His wounds. Yes, partly that was to help them take in the enormity of the situation: it really was Him. The man they had seen crucified was standing in front of them. Yet, I believe there was another, more personal truth that He wanted to share with them.

Throughout his life on earth Jesus was wounded many times before he got to the cross. His family, His disciples, His own people rejected Him or doubted Him time and time again. However, He never let a wound harden his heart. He allowed people to hurt Him again and again, and ultimately received the spear in His heart, knowing that His Father would glorify every wound.

Jesus did not let anything disturb His peace. He would not defend Himself, or boast about His achievements. He never allowed His true position to protect Him. He bore His wounds with patience and without bitterness. This lifestyle He followed through to the cross, where He would ask the Father to forgive those who were torturing and killing Him.

So on the day of His victory He came quietly to His disciples and said, "Peace". They had been afraid, distraught, devastated, disillusioned. Yet here He stood. Death was defeated, the way of the Lamb had conquered.

He wanted them to know that He is the Prince of Peace, not of war. That Love wins. That what was needed wasn't the loud clamour of a victory parade, but a gentle, humble army of lovers to go into the world as He had done.

He showed the disciples His wounds and then told them that in the same way the Father sent Him, He was now sending them. In effect He was saying, *Go and be wounded.* And yet, as they looked at His wounds, they were not horrified. The Scripture says that they were glad when they saw the Lord. Something had happened to those terrible wounds; resurrection had happened. Resurrection had transformed the wounds from marks of torture to marks of love.

Jesus had tried to tell them before: *"I am sending you out like sheep among wolves".*[8]

Now He had demonstrated in His own body what happens to the sheep when a wolf gets hold of it. *As the Father has sent me, even so I am sending you. Terrible and wonderful words.*

An army of wounded lovers?

The invitation is there. Will we join His army of wounded lovers? In some ways if we are believers surrendering to God is, we know, part of the deal. We know it is right, and we battle with ourselves to do just that. The more we discover and experience His overwhelming love for us, the easier it becomes.

---

8. Matthew 10:16

However, the conflict grows more intense when we discover that surrender to God often involves a surrender to people as well. People who are unjust, unfair, unrighteous. When Jesus surrendered to His Father's will, He also appeared to surrender to the Pharisees and to the Romans. He certainly gave Himself into their hands.

He calls us to do the same. It is the way of faith. ***(A) gentle tongue can break a bone.***[9]

How can that be? Can we believe that Love always wins? When we are wounded can we stay gentle, refusing to justify ourselves? What if the enemy is gaining the upper hand? Should we stay quiet?

There are no easy answers, and we must remember that Jesus was at times angry. He took violent action in the temple. Yet it seems that act was an exception in His life. How then can we know how to be lions who are lambs, like our Lord? I think we get at least some clues coming back to the passage we've been looking at in John 20.

New creation

On that resurrection day, Jesus breathed into His disciples in an act of re-creation saying, "***Receive the Holy Spirit***".[10] In the book of Genesis we discover that people were created

---

9. Proverbs 25:15

10. John 20:22

through God's word and God's breath. He formed us from the earth, and breathed into us.[11]

We were created to live in perfect harmony ('shalom') with God and with each other. There was no barrier between Adam and Eve, or between them and God. That is, of course, until they sinned. Jesus went into death on the sixth day of the week (Friday), the day in the old creation when God made man. He died as a man like Adam, taking on Himself all the punishment for the sins of the sons and daughters of Adam down through the ages. Then on the first day of the week, the very first day of the new creation, He presented Himself to the disciples as the last Adam, the first man of the new creation.

As in the first creation He spoke a word; this time it was "*Peace be with you*" - that is *shalom, harmony* be restored. Every barrier had again been broken down, Jesus was announcing that the disciples could live in absolute peace with each other and with God. Then He told them how, and as in the first creation He breathed into them, and they received the Holy Spirit.

This act on resurrection day was a foretaste of the day that the Spirit was to come in Jerusalem on the day of Pentecost. Jesus was bringing them back into God, back into the shalom that had existed in the Garden of Eden.

The Holy Spirit is the One who makes us part of this new

---

11. Genesis 1:26 & 2:7

creation. He is the Spirit of Jesus. No one can be born again without Him.[12] He enables us to live in Christ. We still live in the old creation, but have become new.

Therefore, if anyone is in Christ, he is a new creation. The old has passed away; behold, the new has come.[13]

He gives us the same essence as Christ. We are born of the Spirit into a new world. This is the kingdom of heaven. We are now able to pray that the kingdom would come on earth as it is in heaven, because we are of heaven, calling it down to earth. The kingdom has come within us and can come through us into the natural world around.

We are now in Christ. Our real identity is released in our oneness with Him. We still fight with our old nature, and yet, as Paul put it,

So if my behaviour contradicts my desires to do good, I must conclude that it's not my true identity doing it, but the unwelcome intruder of sin hindering me from being who I really am.[14]

Our true nature, our true identity, unfolds more and more as we explore our standing in Christ. He is not struggling with selfishness or pride. He is not confused or discouraged. He

---

12. John 3:5-6
13. 2 Corinthians 5:17
14. Romans 7:20, TPT

is not sick. He is always full of hope, of faith, of love, of joy, of forgiveness. He is the vine, and all this life flows to us as branches. Our part? To remain in the vine.

Is it hard? Of course it is! Everything of the old order scorns this union. Our natural senses tell us that the laws of the kingdom are crazy. Reason is often louder than faith. Our minds can become battlefields. Yet we can have the mind of Christ.[15] We have to continually realign ourselves with heaven:

Set your minds on things that are above, not on things that are on earth. For you have died, and your life is hidden with Christ in God.[16]

We have died. That is the key to freedom. That is the thing that we so easily forget. We have died to the old creation, the old nature. When I start to feel resentful or stressed, when I am struggling with my failure or fear, I have to find that place of freedom again. I died to the old nature. It cannot hold me. I have been crucified with Christ. My new life is hidden with Jesus in the Father by the power of the Holy Spirit.

This life is lamblike. It seems weak to the world, and yet it contains the whole power of God. Only as we 'hide' in Christ will we have wisdom to know when to speak and when to stay silent. Only in this life will we find power to forgive.

---

15. 1 Corinthians 2:16
16. Colossians 3:2-3

Our authority in surrender

In His commissioning in John 20, the Lord reveals the incredible authority that wounded lovers have. He knew He was sending them into a world full of wolves, so He said,

"Receive the Holy Spirit. If you forgive the sins of any, they are forgiven them; if you withhold forgiveness from any, it is withheld".[17]

Did Jesus ever refuse anyone forgiveness? Does He now? The only ones who do not receive forgiveness are the ones who **will not** receive it. His Holy Spirit is in perfect accord with Jesus. Jesus was ordaining His followers as priests to act on His behalf as they were empowered by the Holy Spirit.

We don't need to be trained in a seminary, or wear special robes. We don't need to be called as missionaries or pastors or elders. If we have received the Holy Spirit, each of us has the authority to pronounce forgiveness of sins in Jesus' name. The person we are speaking to may or may not accept what we say, but nevertheless the very real offer is there.

So how can we withhold forgiveness? The only way I can see us doing that is if we do not speak up about what we know to be true. Jonah did not want to speak to the people of Nineveh. We may have our own inhabitants of a personal Nineveh whom we do not want to see repent. Or we may

---

17. john 20:22-23

battle with shyness, which I believe is not a personality trait, but a sin if it is blocking us from speaking at the prompting of the Holy Spirit. It could be laziness or preoccupation with this world that keeps us quiet. It could be low self-esteem or false teaching. Whatever the obstacle, as we breathe in the Holy Spirit, He will deal with it.

Our part is not to make ourselves perfect, but to fix our eyes on the Perfect One and let Him do His work. We are a new creation. We are in Christ. Let the truth set us free!

All of this helps us to wield the ultimate weapon of a surrendered life: intercession.

Intercession

Intercession is the power that links heaven and earth. It is a revolution that brings the kingdom of heaven onto the earth now. It is dynamic and unstoppable. We join with the Lamb, who is at this moment in heaven interceding for us.[18] We co-operate too with the Holy Spirit, who is the great intercessor on earth.[19] In doing so, we bring the whole power of God into the focus of the intercession.

So what is intercession? Intercession is more than a prayer. More than a lot of prayers. It is taking responsibility for something. It is action more than words. It is identification

---

18. Romans 8:34; Hebrews 7:25
19. Romans 8:26-27

with the one for whom we intercede. It is embracing a cost on their behalf. Jesus' whole life on earth, from the incarnation to the crucifixion, and even to His resurrection and ascension, was one of intercession. He embraced the cost and brought us into the good of everything that He has. He did not hold anything back.

Intercession is a surrendered life poured out. We don't choose what we will intercede for. It is a deposit of love that has come from the heart of the Lamb to His lambs. Jesus' heart is full of love and full of longing for a lost world. He is always looking for those He can share this love with:

"And I sought for a man among them who should build up the wall and stand in the breach before me for the land, that I should not destroy it, but I found none".[20]

When He does find a willing heart, He shares a little part of His love and His longing for a particular person, people, or situation. It is the deepest fellowship that we can possibly know with the Lord on this earth. As sons and daughters we become co-workers, sharing something of His passion, His suffering and His victory for the things with which He trusts us.

To do that we need to let go of our own passions, thoughts, desires. Even our own ideas of how to serve Him. Only His love will enable us to stand for people in the evil

---

20. Ezekiel 22:30

day (and the evil day is here and is coming), and having done everything, still to stand.

The powers with which we contend will not move with a few prayers. Only intercession is powerful enough. An intercession may express itself in prayer, in tears, in fasting, in serving, in forgiving, or in persevering when all hope is lost. It is the real 'holy war'. Just as in physical warfare, we cannot dictate how long it will last. We must just keep pouring ourselves out until the battle is won.

> *Even if I am to be poured out as a drink offering upon the sacrificial offering of your faith, I am glad and rejoice with you all.*[21]

Paul carried an intercession for the churches he had planted, and for the lands yet to hear the gospel. Yet even in the depths of the sacrifice he could rejoice. He was in fellowship with Jesus. He was drawing not on his own resources but the energy of Christ:

> *Him we proclaim, warning everyone and teaching everyone with all wisdom, that we may present everyone mature in Christ. For this I toil, **struggling with all his energy** that he powerfully works within me.*[22]

---

21. Philippians 2:17
22. Colossians 1:28-29, emphasis added

To enable us to hold this love, this intercession, the Lamb has to break our selfish hearts. They are not big enough as they are. Everyone who surrenders to the Lamb will be broken. He puts the broken bread in our hands, as he did with his disciples. He says, **This is my body, given for you; now, feed my sheep.** Don't eat first and then give the leftovers to those who are waiting. You break the bread in your own hands; your bodies, like mine, must be broken for the life of the world.

Only as we are broken will we see the miracles of multiplication. This is how the new wave of life will come. Selfish hearts yielding to his selfless life.

He has given us hearts of flesh, and flesh is made for sacrifice. We cannot bear the sins of the world; that is done, once, for all by the Lamb of God. However, as we follow the Lamb, we can choose to suffer with Him, so that the world might hear and know Him. This is intercession. This was Paul's joy:

*Now I rejoice in my sufferings for your sake, and in my flesh **I am filling up what is lacking** in Christ's afflictions for the sake of his body, that is, the church, of which I became a minister according to the stewardship from God that was given to me for you, **to make the word of God fully known.**[23]*

If this weren't in the Bible we would probably call it heresy! Make up what is lacking in Christ's afflictions! Was anything lacking? Only the making it known: our part. That is our

---

23. Colossians 1:24-25, emphasis added

invitation into the fellowship of His suffering.

The Lamb is more than a conqueror! Our battle is to believe it and to demonstrate our faith in a daily surrender. This surrender will make us more than conquerors too. This surrender is our ultimate secret weapon!

A personal surrender

I grew up on a diet of love stories from teenage magazines and Sunday afternoon films. From as far back as five years old I had crushes on the boy next door or in my class at school. Like many girls, my talk with my friends was filled with boys, and finding that one who would sweep me off my feet.

When I became a Christian I thought I had given 'all that' to the Lord. I still assumed I would get married and have a family, only now I believed I was trusting the Lord to show me who my future partner would be.

I didn't realise that something had got hold of me through those years of 'dreaming' of Mr Right. I had trained my mind and my heart to look out for my future partner. I had filled my thoughts with daydreams, and they would not easily be shifted. In fact, I believe that the enemy came in on this weakness in my life and held ground.

When I was living in North Africa a close friend who was part of the same mission came to visit. She had been sent by our leader who had a concern for me growing in his spirit. We prayed together and began to identify this area that the Lord wanted me to surrender. Actually, when it came to the crunch point, I discovered that what was holding me was a devotion to worldly happiness.

The Lord unveiled the fact that though I was not acting on my desires, so much of my thought life was still spent daydreaming, and wondering if this one or that one was the right one for me. I was shocked as this became clear. I repented and was, I believe, set free from a stronghold that the enemy had built.

A few weeks later the Lord spoke to me again. He asked me if I trusted Him as my Father. When I replied that I did, He showed me how, in the nation in which I was working, most marriages were still arranged by fathers. He asked, *Will you allow Me to choose whether you marry or not? Will you trust that I know you better than you know yourself?*

It was a difficult time. I could not answer Him immediately. I knew that the Lord was asking me to surrender my future happiness to Him. He was asking me to give up my choices, and trust His, whether that was for a husband or not. I struggled for three days. I was in my mid-twenties, and could not easily contemplate a life without a partner. The issue came down to trust. The Lord had captured the heart of the battle in His simple questions to me. Would I trust Him? I think every surrender comes down to this.

So after three days I was left with that simple question: Who would I chose to trust: the Lord or myself? In the starkness of that choice I knew which way I must go. I gave in to His gentle patience with me. I fell into the loving arms of my Father and told Him, Yes! I would trust Him.

The immediate relief was amazing! I felt a pressure lift from me that I now realise I had carried most of my life. I remember laughing in wonder at the freedom of giving God control.

I write now 35 years later, and though I have had my struggles and challenges, I have never regretted that decision. The Lord has kept me single, and has led me into a life that I could never have had if I had been married with children. I see His love and wisdom, and I still rejoice in the freedom of allowing Him to control this area of my life.

I don't in any way hold myself up as an example of a totally surrendered life; I just share this area with you. I continue to discover other areas that I must battle to surrender to Him. Yet I know that as I surrender, I will find greater and greater freedom and joy.

Epilogue

As a new believer when I was 20, I remember struggling to know what my gifts or talents were. One day I felt the Lord ask me, *What do you enjoy doing?* I told him that I enjoyed writing to people. He asked, *Will you give that to me?* I did.

Looking back, I think I stumbled across something of the beautiful simplicity of God. We can strive to do something great for Him, yet He simply asks us, as He asked Moses, ***"What is that in your hand?"***[1] A wooden staff became something the Lord used to part a sea. Giving Him back what He has given us transforms it and transforms us. We are no longer just something from the earth, but heaven comes into all that we give Him.

I have written this book through a time of struggle in my own life. It has helped to ground me again in God's intimate and infinite love. My hope is that in some small way it has done the same for you. Lawlessness is growing throughout

---

1. Exodus 4:2

the world. I recently heard news from a friend in the Middle East, of a nominal Christian taken and beaten by a Muslim family because they did not like his innocent friendship with their daughter. They kept him captive for several days and tortured him. His jaw was broken and he was forced to sign blank cheques, so that they could take all his money. He is the only provider for his family. There is no recourse for him in a court, simply because he is a Christian.

War continues to devastate the helpless, and refugees outnumber residents in many areas of the world. I heard of a Muslim man on one border sewing his mouth closed as a protest. His desperate yet eloquent action speaking louder than any words could, that closed borders were killing him and his family.

Children are growing up knowing nothing but war, deprivation and hatred. The desperation of lawlessness can indeed make love grow cold, as Jesus prophesied. Yet the Lord has not turned His back on His wayward creation. He is the Beloved Warrior.

> *Behold my servant, whom I uphold,*
> *my chosen, in whom my soul delights;*
> *I have put my Spirit upon him;*
> *he will bring forth justice to the nations.*
> *He will not cry aloud or lift up his voice,*
> *or make it heard in the street;*
> *a bruised reed he will not break,*

and a faintly burning wick he will not quench;
he will faithfully bring forth justice.
He will not grow faint or be discouraged
till he has established justice in the earth;
and the coastlands wait for his law.[2]

His warfare is full of mercy, full of healing, because the weapon is love. He woos us, through our bruising, and breathes onto us when our flame is dying. He longs for us to know that we are His beloved. He is never discouraged, and as we stand into His love, so we too will discover that we are warriors. His love, His power, flows through us.

In the next chapter the prophet Isaiah foresaw an incredible thing. He prophesied that the parting of the Red Sea would be as nothing compared with the new thing that the Lord would do. All Jews look back to that tremendous miracle year after year at the Passover. It is at the heart of their faith. Yet Isaiah specifically refers to that event and tells them:

"Remember not the former things,
nor consider the things of old.
Behold, I am doing a new thing;
now it springs forth, do you not perceive it?
I will make a way in the wilderness
and rivers in the desert.
The wild beasts will honour me,

---

2. Isaiah 42:1-4

the jackals and the ostriches,
for I give water in the wilderness,
rivers in the desert,
to give drink to my chosen people".[3]

There would be a time when the wilderness of this world would be transformed. A time when even the wild beasts, those people whom it seemed would never bow the knee, would honour God. It would be a new thing, yet it was already springing forth in Israel's hope for a Messiah.

Jesus, the Messiah, when He came announced the fulfilment of Isaiah's prophecy when he cried out,

"Whoever believes in me, as the Scripture has said, 'Out of his heart will flow rivers of living water.'" Now this he said about the Spirit, whom those who believed in him were to receive, for as yet the Spirit had not been given, because Jesus was not yet glorified.[4]

This was the new thing! It is a continually new thing. Every time we believe Jesus we become transformers. We have the ability to make any desert bloom. Jesus announced this truth on the last and greatest day of the Feast of Tabernacles. This feast is the one to which all nations are commanded to come. Isaiah saw that there would be something greater than the salvation of a nation; it would be that same offer of salvation to all who would believe, in every nation of the world.

---

3. Isaiah 43:18-20

4. John 7:38-39

This new thing is continual, ongoing, creative. We are the new thing! The Spirit living in us is the new thing. We can stand with our loving warrior King and pour out our lives to see the wildest and most barren places blossom. We have a choice. Will we be overwhelmed by this world, or will we be those who will allow our hearts to break and overflow to bring heaven's life-giving water to those who may not even realise that they are dying of thirst?

"What is that in your hand?"

Acknowledgements

Rowland Evans, the founder of both World Horizons and Nations, and my spiritual father. You helped me to build a strong foundation and gave me confidence to step out in faith. It would be hard to exaggerate the godly influence you have had in my life.

Kathy Coupe for your friendship, your insights and your help in editing this book.

Robert Reeve for your encouragement, wisdom and advice.

Les and Pilar Norman, you always knew when I was needing encouragement, even though I was out of sight. Thanks for your help and prayer.

Darryl and Joy Greig, you inspire me by your commitment

to truth lived out. Thanks for all your helpful comments.

Those I have worked with over the years in Europe, Africa, the Middle East and Asia. You are my heroes and my inspiration to keep pressing forward into Jesus and His calling.

All monies raised from the sale of this book will go to support the work of **Nations Trust.**

For more information about Nations, Celebration for the Nations or World Horizons please see the links below:

www.nations.org.uk
www.celebrationforthenations.org
www.worldhorizons.co.uk

Handwritten notes:

Time travel Seriel

living in to benefits of another era (time)

Hungary for the company of those who live in a different spiritual atmosphere

Printed in Poland
by Amazon Fulfillment
Poland Sp. z o.o., Wrocław